THE FOOL .

The Fool

0

Tarot

For Beginners

A Practical Guide to Reading the Cards

Lisa Novak

About the Author

Tarot has been a part of Barbara Moore's personal and professional lives for nearly twenty years. Right from the start, tarot intrigued her with its marvelous blending of mythology, psychology, art, history, mystery, and magic. She has studied under renowned tarot scholars such as Mary K. Greer and Rachel Pollack, and continues to work with some of the brightest lights in the tarot world. Currently, she consults for both Llewellyn Worldwide and Lo Scarabeo, is one of the founders of the Minnesota Area Tarot Symposium (http://minnesotatarot.com/), is an enthusiastic and active member of the Twin Cities Tarot Meetup group, performs readings at a local haunted house, and consults the cards every chance she gets. She teaches tarot locally, nationally, and internationally.

Her website can be found here:

http://www.practicaltarotreadings.com

Tarot

For Beginners

A Practical Guide to Reading the Cards

BARBARA MOORE

Llewellyn Publications
Woodbury, Minnesota

FIRST EDITION
First Printing, 2010

Book design and editing by Rebecca Zins

Cover design by Adrienne W. Zimiga

Library of Congress Cataloging-in-Publication Data
Moore, Barbara, 1963–
 Tarot for beginners : a practical guide to reading the cards / Barbara Moore.—1st ed.
   p. cm.
 Includes bibliographical references.
 ISBN 978-0-7387-1955-9
 1. Tarot. I. Title.
 BF1879.T2M6525 2010
 133.3'2424—dc22

                                                            2010025299

Llewellyn Publications
A Division of Llewellyn Worldwide Ltd.
2143 Wooddale Drive
Woodbury, MN 55125-2989
www.llewellyn.com

Printed in the United States of America

Other Books by Barbara Moore

A Guide to Mystic Faerie Tarot
(Mystic Faerie Tarot; art by Linda Ravenscroft)

The Gilded Tarot Companion
(Gilded Tarot; art by Ciro Marchetti)

The Witchy Tarot
(The Hip Witch Tarot; art by Antonella Platano
and concept by Laura Tuan)

Destiny's Portal
(Enchanted Oracle; art by Jessica Galbreth)

The Dreamer's Journal
(The Mystic Dreamer Tarot; art by Heidi Darras)

The Pagan Tarot
(The Pagan Magical Kit; art by Luca Raimondo and
Cristiano Spadoni, concept by Gina Pace)

The Vampires of the Eternal Night Tarot (art by David Corsi)

The Tarot of the Sweet Twilight (art by Cristina Benintende)

The Dream Enchantress Tarot (art by Marco Nizzoli)

Shadowscapes Companion
with Stephanie Pui-Mun Law
(Shadowscapes Tarot; art by Stephanie Pui-Mun Law)

For Lisa, who has the courage to foster greatness by whatever means necessary.

Acknowledgments

Heartfelt thanks to all the tarot lovers who came before me, who traveled with me, and who are yet to come. Special thanks to Theresa Reed, who was there when I needed help finding my way, and to Catherine Chapman, who never failed to make me feel like a rock star. Becky, you have a magic touch with both words and design; thank you for making my work better than it was. And to Lynne Menturweck, your precise skill is, as always, much appreciated.

Contents

Introduction

Everyone who reads the cards has a memory of the first time they saw a deck. My memory is vague and murky, but this is how I remember it: I was very young, maybe about six or eight years old. My mother took me to visit her great aunt. I don't remember why; we didn't have much to do with my mother's family, who had come to Detroit from Sicily by way of Louisiana. We drove from the suburbs into Detroit, a slightly frightening journey even back then. We went into this dark room, heavy with weird vibes and incense, where my aunt sat, cards nearby. There was strange talk that I didn't understand, and cards were shuffled, followed by whispered questions and answers. Although my mother's family was steeped in spiritualism, the occult arts, and eclectic voodoo, except for that one elusive memory, I did not have further contact with the cards for many years.

That next contact, however, sealed the deal. My college roommate and I threw a party, and during the course of that party, she pulled out a deck of cards. She didn't read with them but handed them around for people to look at. For me, it was love at first sight. Although I wasn't quite sure what each card meant or even what exactly one was supposed to do with them, I looked in the tiny paper booklet that came with the deck, shuffled the cards, carefully laid them out, and started reading with them.

After that, I purchased or borrowed every tarot book I could get my hands on and collected different decks. Even though I knew the cards were just pieces of paper with pictures on them, I knew that they (and what they represented) were much more. I knew that through the cards, secrets could be revealed, and I could discover entire worlds.

Twenty years later, I am happy to say that I was right. Even better, now I get to show you how to use the cards to unveil mysteries and uncover secrets. I started my tarot journey by jumping right in, which was exhilarating in its own way. But after that initial leap, I was glad to have good books to help me become a more skilled reader. And that's the goal of this book: to help you become a confident reader in the easiest, most efficient way possible—while having some fun too!

How will we do that, you wonder? Here's the plan. First, we'll take a peek into the background of the cards themselves. Where did these cards come from, anyhow? Is their history really shrouded in mystery? Next, we'll look at each card, one by one, and discover their meanings. Doing a tarot reading is a lot like reading a book. Before you can read a novel, you have to master your ABCs, and so it is with tarot: the cards are like your new alphabet.

Learning the cards is the first step, but you don't go right from singing the alphabet song directly to writing *War and Peace*. Being able to make words and create sentences comes next. So before we jump into doing full readings, we'll see how the cards work together to create more complex and precise meanings.

Then we'll put it all together, shuffle the cards, lay them out, and see what amazing revelations are revealed.

While it is true that tarot is fun, there is a more serious side, too. You will find that in tarot there are not many hard and fast rules that must be followed; there are always different ways to do almost anything. Many teachers will tell you that it comes down to personal preference if, for example, you want to read reversed cards or let someone else handle your cards. That is true—up to a point. But really, I think it is more than merely personal preference. The power of the tarot and the truth we find in our readings comes from *somewhere*. Where? Well, the truth is that no one knows for sure, and each reader must decide for herself the answer to that question. And that answer will help you make choices as you develop your personal reading style. Don't worry or stress about this, though. You don't have to know the answer before you start. In most cases, the answer reveals itself to each person as they learn. And sometimes the answer evolves over time and can take your tarot practice into completely new directions.

Are you ready to plumb the mysteries of the universe, divine your future, and understand the secrets of your soul? Yes?

Okay, then. Let's begin what I am sure will be a fabulous journey.

I: Basics

Tarot cards are really amazing in so many ways. For one, you will be glad to know it is not difficult to understand the basics of the deck and of reading the cards. The process breaks down into very logical parts that build on each other. Go through the steps, and you'll be reading before you know it.

Learning to read the cards has a lot in common with learning to read. First you learn the alphabet, then you put the ABCs together to create words; the words create sentences, and so on. Once you have the basic foundation, you continually add to your vocabulary and become more skillful in adding nuance and precision to your written and spoken communication. You can then take language in any direction and do any number of things with it: write poetry, tell amazing stories, communicate information, sing. Reading the cards follows much the same path. You learn basics. Your cards become your alphabet. Your readings become your essays. Your reading style becomes your novel, poem, or song.

Before going somewhere new, it is usually helpful to look at a map. Once you have an idea of the lay of the land, it is much easier to see how the individual elements work together. This chapter is packed with lots of interesting information that will help you begin creating the map for your journey into the world of tarot. Because so many subjects have their own jargon, let's start with a glossary so we are all speaking the same language. A short history lesson is necessary as well—not so much that you know who did what when, but more so that you understand tarot's fluid nature. And then we'll get to what is for many the main feature of tarot: what makes a reading a reading.

Part of the reason you are reading this book, I hope, is to learn what the cards mean. We can make that process a lot easier by understanding the structure of a deck and breaking it down into smaller, more manageable bits. And, since you are going on a journey, it is wise to keep a record of the experience. Hence, we end this jam-packed chapter with ideas for keeping a journal.

Glossary

Arcana: A secret or mystery.

Court cards: The sixteen cards of the Minor Arcana named page, knight, queen, and king.

Divination: The act of divining; predicting the future or interpreting messages from the Divine. Traditionally, divination is the act of telling the future. Modern tarotists use the term to mean communication with the Divine.

Divine: Not a tarot term but used in this book to mean God, the universe, Great Spirit, Higher Self, higher power, etc.

Fortunetelling: Predicting the future.

Golden Dawn: A secret magical society that existed in England at the end of the nineteenth and beginning of the twentieth centuries. Arthur E. Waite (creator of the Rider-Waite-Smith

Tarot) and Aleister Crowley (creator of the Thoth Tarot) were members.

Major Arcana: The twenty-two cards in a tarot deck, numbered 0–XXI.

Minor Arcana: The fifty-six cards in a tarot deck, divided into four suits and numbered ace through ten, plus the court cards.

Predictive: As in a predictive reading—a reading in which the future is foretold.

Prescriptive: As in a prescriptive reading—a reading in which the focus is on giving the querent advice.

Qabalah: A Western esoteric and mystical tradition drawing on Jewish Kabbalah (Jewish mysticism), astrology, alchemy, and other mystical studies.

Querent: In a reading, the querent is the person asking the question. If someone is reading for herself, she is both the reader and the querent.

Reader: In a reading, the reader is the person conducting the reading and interpreting the cards.

Reading: Using the cards to discover information.

Situation: In this book, "the situation" or "this situation" refers to the situation that the reading is about, also known as the question.

Spread: The way the cards are laid out in order to be interpreted. Most spreads include specific meanings for each position, but some spreads do not use positional meanings.

Tarotist: A tarot reader, scholar, or enthusiast.

Tarot Fact and Fancy

If you read other tarot books (and I would certainly encourage you to do so), you will find that including a chapter on the history of tarot is practically a requirement. Some people love that aspect of learning tarot; others aren't so interested. And that's fine. It's not necessary to take a history lesson to read tarot. However, having a nodding acquaintance with tarot's story has one benefit—it will help you understand how significantly tarot has changed over the years. This is a particularly important point, because it is too tempting to pretend that the tarot and the meanings of the cards are absolute. There are some people who say, "Oh, that's not what the cards mean" or "That book is wrong." There are others who say, "We must go back to the writings of so-and-so from the eighteenth century, because those are the true meanings." This brief section will show you how tarot has evolved and continues to evolve, reflecting our ideas of truth and adapting to our beliefs as society and as individuals.

Although tarot constantly changes, one thing that has remained constant about the cards is the idea of stories. We humans love stories, and fortunately for us, the history of tarot is full of great ones. For example, tucked away in museums are a few decks that were created in the fifteenth century—miniature works of art dripping with gold leaf. One of these decks was commissioned as a wedding gift. It is said that some of the figures in the cards resemble the bride and the groom.

Another story is that at one time, it was believed that the cards came from the pyramids in distant and mysterious Egypt, a gift from the Egyptian god Thoth, given to humankind centuries ago but lost to obscurity. Luckily, a few eighteenth-century Europeans "re-discovered" this gift and gave it back to the world.

Some have said that the Gypsies (who were named after but not actually from Egypt) brought tarot cards to Europe, demanding that their palms be crossed with silver. In exchange for the silver, they turned over the cards slowly, spinning tales of both good fortune and woe.

Tarot cards have been condemned as "the devil's picture book"—although why the devil would picture himself in such an unflattering manner and include an image of the pope and the holy grail is a mystery.

These stories and more have been told about the tarot. If you are interested in reading more, Rachel Pollack compiled a wonderful collection in her book *Forest of Souls*. Whether we think the stories are true or not is beside the point; they are still part of its history, part of its mythology. They are part of why the tarot, after all this time, still holds the power to enchant and inspire us. Stories, fables, fairy tales, myths, jokes, movies … these are all ways we teach and learn lessons, ways we make sense of the world. And the cards themselves are used to tell stories. We shuffle the cards, lay them down, and read them, just as we would a story. Are the stories we read in the cards any more or any less true than any other stories we tell? Well, perhaps it is that they are *all* true, in their own way—because, really, the stories we tell say more about *us* than they do the actual subject of the story. The lines dividing truth, fact, and history from story, myth, and dream are not always clear.

The story most tarotists currently tell about the history of tarot is based on the available historical evidence—account books, receipts, laws, letters, and existing cards. Using this data, we feel confident in saying that tarot cards showed up in Europe in the fifteenth century. These hand-painted cards were used by noble families to play a card game called *tarrochi*, a trick-taking game similar to bridge. Sadly, there is no evidence suggesting that they were considered magical or used for hiding secret teachings. They were illustrated with images and symbols that would have been familiar to any European of the day, because they incorporated scenes and characters that appeared in stained glass windows all over Europe.

While there is some evidence that tarot and playing cards were used to tell fortunes in the sixteenth century, it wasn't until the eighteenth century that tarot became fully immersed in the esoteric world. A pastor named Antoine Court de Gébelin was the first that we know of to claim an occult connection with the cards. He associated a card with a letter of the Hebrew alphabet, and thus the connection between tarot and Qabalah was born. Later, a Parisian seed salesman, Jean-Baptiste Alliette (who wrote under the name Etteilla, which is "Alliette" spelled backwards), created the first deck specifically for divination, but it was quite different from existing tarot decks. In the nineteenth century, secret societies abounded, and through them tarot was connected with all sorts of things, such as alchemy, Qabalah, and astrology. In 1909, Golden Dawn member Arthur E. Waite published, through Rider & Company, his deck with images painted by Pamela (Pixie) Colman Smith, now known as the Rider-Waite or Rider-Waite-Smith Tarot and one of the most important decks ever created. In 1943, Aleister Crowley and artist Lady Frieda Harris completed the Thoth Tarot, which wasn't published until 1969 and is still popular with readers. However, for whatever reason, the Rider-Waite-Smith Tarot (hereafter RWS) has become the standard, particularly in the United States. Most beginners learn with this deck, and a majority of decks published today are based on the RWS tradition even though it was not the first tarot deck ever designed or even the first designed for divination.

In the early twentieth century, tarot was primarily used in two ways. The Gypsy fortuneteller approach was common and gave rise to some popular Hollywood ideas about tarot readers, including proclamations about tall dark strangers, perilous journeys over water, and sudden death. Secret societies used the cards as placeholders for esoteric knowledge and spiritual belief systems. Using the cards in this way has shaped the modern tarot practice of correspondences, which we'll discuss in chapter 2. After the start of World War I, interest in tarot waned.

That waning interest reignited in the 1960s. Eden Gray's books *The Tarot Revealed* and *Mastering the Tarot* became the first about tarot that many novice tarotists read at the time. Gray's work was an amalgamation of Gypsy fortuneteller meanings and secret society practices, and she influenced many of today's most celebrated tarotists. In the 1970s, people who learned from Gray went on to change tarot in ways that affect how readers, students, and authors view tarot even today. And by the mid-1980s, two women published works that are among the most loved tarot books of the last twenty years. Rachel Pollack published *78 Degrees of Wisdom*, two volumes of in-depth study of card meanings weaving together esotericism, mythology, and psychology. Mary K. Greer published *Tarot for Your Self*, which teaches how to read the cards for personal insight and psychological transformation.

Although there are still old-school fortunetellers around—and, indeed, they are making a comeback—psychology has become both the lens through which the cards are viewed and the way the cards are used. Like any other lens, it has benefits and downsides. This approach is usually considered more intelligent and less scary than fortunetelling. It leads to self-understanding. It supports the philosophy of free will and shuns that of deterministic fate. It empowers the querent and encourages a proactive approach to life. There are, however, a growing number of readers who believe that providing information about future events does *not* inhibit free will—rather, that it empowers querents to intelligently plan for whatever lies ahead. One of the main downsides of the psychological approach is that after about three decades of psychological expansion, each card has been said to mean so many things that it is overwhelming and almost impossible to definitively say what a card actually means. Also, by assuming the psychological approach is the only correct one, the tarot community is in danger of becoming stagnant, as Rachel Pollack herself observed in *Llewellyn's 2007 Tarot Reader*:

> If the psychological method of tarot works so well, why not stay with it? Certainly it has not exhausted its usefulness. And yet, whenever something becomes standard, or accepted without questioning, I begin to get nervous. What are we missing? What have we found? What have we stopped ourselves from finding? And so, I have begun to think that just as modern readers rescued the tarot from fortunetelling a quarter century ago, it might be time to rescue it from its new master, psychology.

From a game to secret occult teachings to Gypsy stereotypes to therapy, tarot has played many roles. Societies and individuals have looked into the mirror that is tarot, and the reflections have revealed changes in culture and in individuals. Through the years, tarot—sometimes called the "royal road"—followed a path rich with entertainment, mystery, wisdom, and beauty. And each of us who ever shuffle a deck take part in that ongoing journey, both shaping and being shaped by it.

Readings

I love the way tarot cards feel in my hands as I shuffle them. I love tapping them back into a neat pack after gathering them up. I love the pictures on them. I love that they are practical. How many little, fairly inexpensive treasures do you own that not only please the senses but also provide advice and wisdom about your life? And really, for most people, this practical application, which we call "reading the cards" or "doing a reading," is the most basic reason we are drawn to tarot. Knowing a little bit of what lies ahead and how to face it is something we all value, but the fact that it can come in such a pleasing package is a bonus.

Learning to read the cards is not difficult. The hardest thing, really, is understanding that for every aspect of tarot, there is no absolute right or wrong way to do anything. In this chapter, you'll learn the basic outline of a reading. In later chapters, you will explore ways to create your own unique reading style and add precision to your work.

A tarot reading is the act of interpreting the cards. Whether you use the cards to predict the future, to solve a problem, or to understand yourself better, you accomplish each of those through a doing a reading. All that is needed is a reader, a querent, a question, a spread, and, of course, a deck of tarot cards.

The reader is the person who performs the reading and can be someone who is shuffling a deck for the first time or someone who has studied the tarot for years and years. You can be a reader right this minute, even if you've never read before. You don't believe me? Try this: if you have a deck, shuffle it, ask "What message does the tarot have for me right now?" and pull one card. If you don't have a deck, flip through this book, stopping randomly at a page with pictures of cards on it. Look at the picture (whether on the card you selected or on the page you stopped at), and tell a story about what you see. Don't worry about the words on the cards or any strange images or symbols that you don't recognize. Pretend you are a child who cannot read and is looking at a picture book, making up stories. Turn your story into a message. There: you have just performed your first reading.

If you did the reading described above, you were both the reader and the querent. The querent is the person asking the question. People do read for themselves, although this wasn't always true (and still isn't in many parts of Europe). Some people have concerns about objectivity and think that being too close to or involved in a situation will affect the interpretation. Then again, many people think of the tarot as a mirror that reflects our deepest, truest selves back to us, so reading for ourselves is very useful. And, in any event, all readers bring their own judgments and opinions to any reading they do. In tarot reading, as in journalism, perfect objectivity might not be an obtainable state. Objective or not, in a reading there may be just one person who is both reader and querent or there may be two or more people, a reader and at least one querent.

There is a reason for the reading, usually in the form of a question. In the example above, the question was "What message does the tarot have for me right now?" Most modern readers want the querent to share her question in as much detail as possible. Knowing the question provides the reader another element to use in shaping the interpretation. Other readers ask the querent to think about his question but not verbalize it. Some readers don't have the querent ask a question at all, believing the cards themselves will reveal what the querent needs to know, regardless of what she may want to know. So, technically, we don't need a question to conduct a reading. However, because the reading will provide an answer, there is an assumed question, even if it wasn't verbalized. Whether a question is asked or not, the querent came to the tarot wanting *something*—looking for answers, searching for guidance, or seeking wisdom.

A spread, or a layout, is the way that the cards are laid out. In the reading above, we used a one-card spread, where the single card drawn provides the answer to the question. This one-card spread can be used for any question. However, most readers prefer using three or more cards. Spreads usually instruct us to lay the cards out in a certain order and to assign a meaning to the position that each card holds.

Here is a simple three-card spread:

1. Past influences

2. Present situation

3. Future outcome

We lay out the cards in numerical order and use the positional meaning to mold the interpretation. Some readers use one or only a few different spreads for all readings. Some people use many kinds of spreads or even make them up on the spot. Other readers lay out the cards in rows or columns but do not assign any meanings to the positions. This is more commonly called "laying out the cards," as that is what is being done, as opposed to using a spread. In either case, the cards end up on the table to be interpreted.

None of this matters—reader, querent, question, or spread— if we don't have a deck of tarot cards. There are so many decks available. But before running out and buying one, do some research. Your tarot deck will become your tool, and any good craftsperson will tell you that a high-quality tool that feels good in your hands is important. Without that, doing excellent work is much harder. Take some time and make an informed choice, but don't stress about it too much. If the deck doesn't work out for you, you can try another one. Look for a deck that is labeled "tarot." There are other kinds of oracle decks available, but not all oracle decks are tarot decks. Simply put, an oracle deck is any divination deck that does not say "tarot" in the title or on the box; beyond that, there are no parameters or characteristics shared among oracle decks. They can have any number of cards, any sort of structure (or no structure at all), be based on a theme (such as angels or faeries), or be entirely random. Oracle decks are fine tools, but if you are looking for a deck to use with this book, you'll want to get a tarot deck. Look for a deck that has pictures on all seventy-eight cards. Some will have pictures on about half of the cards, with the other half looking something like playing cards, with just symbols arranged on the card. Decks of this sort are Marseille-style tarot, slightly different from the RWS-style decks we are using for this book. People do read with Marseille decks, but that style isn't best suited for use with this book. Look for a deck that is in the RWS tradition. Most, but not all, modern decks fall into this category. Visit websites that include in-depth reviews of tarot decks. Many of these reviews do include whether or not a deck is RWS-based. See appendix B for deck suggestions and websites. Finally, find a deck that you love to look at and that inspires you.

Ritual

Rituals, while not a necessary part of doing a reading, do play a supportive role if incorporated. They can also be fun and add a theatrical or mysterious touch that many enjoy. Rituals help us calm down, center, and focus on the task at hand. Performing a ritual or rituals before a reading lets the mind know that it is time to get into reading mode. Getting into reading mode usually means toning down the analytical mind and turning up the intuitive mind. Both ways of thinking are important to a reading; however, we spend most of our time in analytical mode. Therefore, before starting a reading, it is beneficial to balance both sides.

Don't be put off by the word "ritual," thinking it means some elaborate, strange, absurd rigmarole. In simplest terms, a ritual is a consistent way of doing things—something as simple and unobtrusive as taking a deep breath and letting it out slowly. On the other hand, if you are drawn to velvet, silk, crystals, and incense, your rituals can be as elaborate as you like. I encourage you to adapt some sort of ritual that is comfortable for you, even if it's just for yourself, especially at first, if you feel a little nervous when doing a reading. Closing your eyes and taking a few deep breaths before beginning a reading is a good way to quiet the mind and calm the nerves. In addition to simply breathing, you can center yourself by pulling your energy inward and calming your mind. Ground yourself by visualizing a connection to the earth, breathing out anxiety and breathing in earth's stable, calming energy. Many readers begin their readings with a prayer or by asking for guidance. If you begin your reading with a prayer, it adds a nice sense of symmetry to end the reading with one as well. Thank the Divine for the guidance provided or ask a blessing upon yourself or your querent.

Since it must be done anyway, shuffling is an easy way to incorporate ritual into a reading. The method of shuffling isn't important; use whatever manner is most comfortable for you. To make it into a ritual, simply use that method every time. Decide how many times (for example, seven times) or for how long you will shuffle (for example, as long as it takes to say a prayer). A fellow tarotist, Barbara Chaitman, uses an interesting method for determining the number of times she will shuffle before a reading. First, she decides the main theme of the reading, and then she matches that theme to one of the Major Arcana cards. For example, if she is doing a relationship reading, she picks VI, the Lovers. If it is about finding inner strength, she picks VIII, Strength. For a reading about moving, she might select VII, the Chariot; for a career, perhaps IV, the Emperor. Then she looks at the number on that card and shuffles that number of times (in the case of our examples, six, eight, seven, or four times, respectively).

Remember that doing anything—breathing, praying, shuffling, etc.—the same way each time is not required. That is to say, a reading is still a reading with or without ritual. But if you want the benefits of ritual—calmness, centeredness, and a balanced and receptive mind and spirit—then simply doing even just one thing the same way every time is sufficient. That is what makes something a ritual, after all.

In addition to the manner of shuffling, you need to decide whether you, as the reader, will be the only one shuffling or if your querents will also shuffle. This may seem like an odd question, but most readers have specific ideas about energy and its role in a reading. This goes back to that original question from the introduction: Where does the power and truth of the tarot come from? How does the tarot work? Is it an interchange of energy between reader and querent, is it a direct connection between the reader and the Divine, or is it a unique and temporary bond between the reader, the querent, and the Divine—or is it something else entirely? If you believe someone else's energy will dilute or interfere with the reading, then you would probably not be inclined to let anyone else shuffle your cards. If you believe that the other person's energy is an important part of how tarot works, then you will likely ask them to shuffle as well.

Cutting the cards is another way to include ritual. Again, any method will work, as long as it is the same every time. A popular technique is to ask the querent to cut the cards in three piles (using their non-dominant hand) and then pick up the piles in any order and restack them. Some readers do not ask querents to shuffle and may or may not ask them to cut the cards.

Once the cards are shuffled and cut, it is time to deal them out. There are two ways to do this (as well as variations), so you have another choice to play around with, and I would suggest trying both before you decide which to stick with. You may even decide to use both, depending on your mood, the reading, or other factors. Dealing the cards face-down and flipping them over one at a time creates a sense of anticipation and mystery. It makes it easier to focus on one card at a time, instead of peeking ahead to see what card is next. Dealing the cards face-up allows a quick scan of the reading that provides certain information that many find useful at the start of a reading (for more on this, see chapter 3). With some spreads, you may find that dealing some of the cards face-down and some face-up works very well.

Dealing the cards from the top of the deck is not the only way to select which ones go into the spread. Try spreading all the cards on the table like a large fan and letting the querent run a hand over the cards, selecting the number needed for the spread based on which cards feel right. The reader (or the querent) can cut the deck into the same number of piles as positions in the spread; place one pile in each position and turn over the top card.

There are other ways to enhance the reading experience or add a sense of ritual, but this is enough for building our broad overview map. We'll discuss the importance of ritual in more detail in chapter 4, as well as other practices that can add to your tarot reading experience.

As you can see, there are many variables to think about and decisions to make when you begin reading the cards. Many of the choices made will be personal preference—perhaps overhand shuffling is simply more comfortable for you than riffling, for one. Some of the choices will be based on personal beliefs. For those using the cards to find spiritual guidance, saying a prayer at the beginning and end might be considered essential, not optional. As important as these decisions can be, there is one that is even more fundamental and often a bit more difficult to make: formulating the question.

Questions

Most of us come to the tarot looking for answers of some sort, and most of us have heard the saying that in order to get the right answer, we have to ask the right question. Asking the question is probably one of the most important aspects of a tarot reading. Right off the bat, the question takes control over the reading by providing the focus of the answer. But the question also does more than that: it is a microcosm of a belief system ... or it should be. Let me show you what I mean.

Let's look at two extreme variations of the same question. What does the question "Will I ever get married?" tell us about the person asking it (besides the obvious assumptions such as they are likely single and that they probably would like to be married)? It also implies that they believe in a predetermined universe where whether or not they will marry has already been decided on some cosmic level. If someone asks, "What can I do to bring love into my life?" we can deduce that they believe they have quite a bit of control over their life. These are, admittedly, extreme versions. I am willing to bet that most of us fall somewhere in the middle.

Being clear on your beliefs helps you to ask questions that reflect what you believe. It will make your readings a more natural fit for your life and an extension of how you operate in the world. Most people these days seem to fall somewhere in the middle of determinism and free will. My favorite way to think about the future and making predictions is to compare it to weather forecasting. By taking into account as many variables as possible and by using certain equations, meteorologists make predictions about weather. Because it is impossible to take into account every variable and to run every possible equation, forecasts are not always 100 percent accurate, and the further out they try to forecast, the less certain the prediction becomes because there is more time for something to happen that can change everything. For me, a tarot reading is very much like a weather forecast. Knowing what is likely to happen helps us be prepared, so that when or if the event occurs, we'll be able to respond in a thoughtful manner.

Although I love the idea of having control over my life and not being a victim of circumstances, I do think that there are things that happen in our lives over which we have little or no control. In the face of these events, we still have the power to react as we choose, and those actions can affect the future. The future is, I think, a fascinating dance between our actions, the actions of others, and the wondrous flow of the universe that blends everything together, creating the reality we experience. That's my view, at least at present. What is important, though, is what constitutes *your* view.

Forming your own questions based on your beliefs will help you find answers using tarot that will be practical for you. While you may (or may not) see the benefit of asking questions in a way that reflects your beliefs, you will certainly want information that will be useful to you. For example, think about the possible answers to your question. Imagine what you will do or how you will feel when you find out the answer. How will it affect your actions or decisions? Why do you want to know? Are you very sure you *really* want to know, no matter what the answer is? After thinking about your original question in this way, you might just come up with a different question entirely—one that, in the end, is more helpful and satisfying than the one you started with.

If you are going to read for others, there is another aspect you will want to think about. If you are being careful to make sure your questions reflect your beliefs, what about the questions of others? Should you help them rephrase their questions so that they reflect your beliefs too? Is it your duty to help them in the best way that you know how, based on your understanding of the universe? Should you read for whatever question they ask, whether or not you think it is a good one? If you don't believe in determinism, and someone asks if they are going to get a job soon, would you even be able to read for that question? If you enjoy a more predictive tarot reading experience, seeking glimpses of the future and possible treasures or dire warnings hiding around the corner, could you read effectively for practical advice, such as "What can I focus on in my yearly review to ensure my salary request is met?"

The tarot is a mirror, and a tarot reading is a reflection of one's worldview, a glimpse of a belief system. This is true whether the reader and the querent are aware of it or not. However, we may as well be aware of our predispositions and use the tarot in a way that complements them rather than works against them. By applying this practice of using the cards in a way that reflects our personal beliefs, we really can't say we don't believe in tarot cards. The tarot cards are just cards, after all. It is how we use them that matters.

Structure

Understanding the structure of a tarot deck provides two benefits. The structure is a tool, both for learning the cards and for interpreting a reading. First, by breaking the seventy-eight cards of a tarot deck into smaller parts, it is easier to learn the cards.

Learning a few groups that follow a simple system is much less overwhelming than trying to identify seventy-eight random cards. Second, in addition to each card's specific meaning, the numbers and suits of the cards work together to provide additional information in a reading. We'll focus on the basic structure here, as an introduction to the cards, and discuss using the structure as part of the interpretation later in chapter 3.

The seventy-eight cards in a tarot deck are divided into two groups: the Major Arcana and the Minor Arcana. *Arcana* means "secret" or "mystery," so the Major Arcana are the greater mysteries and the Minor Arcana are the smaller mysteries. Twenty-two of the cards make up the Major Arcana. These cards are numbered 0–XXI and also have names, such as 0, the Fool; VI, the Lovers; and XVII, the Star. Some decks may use arabic numbers for the Major Arcana, but usually roman numerals are favored. Most decks use the same names and numerical order, though some decks do switch VIII, Strength and XI, Justice and use VIII, Justice and XI, Strength instead. In addition, some decks change the names of some cards, particularly XIII, Death, to something like XIII, Transformation. But the majority of decks will use Major Arcana names and numbers that are recognizable and comparable to those used in this book. These cards, the Major Arcana, except 0, the Fool, are the trump cards in the game of tarrochi—cards that are able to take tricks and alter the direction of play. They are also trumps in a tarot reading, playing the same role in a reading as they do in the card game. They represent important events in our lives, often ones that are considered beyond our control and able to change the direction of our lives in new, unexpected, and exciting ways. This is why they are called the greater mysteries.

The Major Arcana cards play another interesting role. For a few decades now, many tarotists consider the Major Arcana a map of the psychological and spiritual journey that all humans experience. Comparable to the Hero's Journey written about by Joseph Campbell, this journey through the tarot cards is called the Fool's Journey. In this journey, 0, the Fool card, travels through all the other Major Arcana until reaching the final card, XXI, the World, where he is said to begin his journey again.

The remaining fifty-six cards are called the Minor Arcana, the smaller mysteries. The cards of the Minor Arcana represent the events of our everyday lives. These cards are divided into four suits, much like a deck of playing cards. The suits are commonly called wands, cups, swords, and pentacles, although sometimes deck designers use alternate names such as rods, chalices, spears, and coins. Each suit has an ace through ten, as well as four court cards, generally called king, queen, knight, and page. These court cards are sometimes renamed using other systems such as father, mother, son, and daughter.

Over the years, each of the four suits has become associated with an elemental energy. The elemental energies are based on the classical Greek idea that the world is made of four basic elements: fire, air, water, and earth. Even though we know the world is made up of many more much smaller elements, tarotists still use this division. Like everything else in tarot, it is a metaphor. This book follows the current trend of using the following associations:

Wands = Fire

Cups = Water

Swords = Air

Pentacles = Earth

Some decks reverse the associations for wands and swords.

Elemental associations are used to represent the realms of life that each suit governs. The suit of wands/fire includes what we would think of as fiery energy—passionate, energetic, inspiring, and dangerous—and governs projects and careers. Cups/water covers emotions, relationships, dreams, intuition, the soul, and the subconscious. Swords/air has long been associated with problems; take a look at the suit of swords and see for yourself. More specifically, though, swords represent logic, thinking, and communication. Faulty thinking or a breakdown in communication certainly can cause problems. Pentacles/earth energy is grounded, stable, and prosperous, and is pertinent to the physical world, finances, resources, and health.

The aces through tens show events that happen in day-to-day life. The court cards, as part of the Minor Arcana, also represent aspects of our everyday lives, although they are not usually read as events but as people. I hesitate to say this, but I must, for you will more than likely hear it somewhere else anyway: it is generally accepted that the court cards are the most difficult to interpret. There are several reasons why this is true. First, kings, queens, knights, and pages don't really play relevant roles in our lives. Second, the card images usually don't provide much help, because they are usually vague images of someone sitting or standing but not really doing anything. Third, traditionally (in fortunetelling) they represented people based on gender, age, skin, hair, and eye color. Later, astrological associations were included. Because the traditional appearance system didn't include all combinations, the interpretations evolved into a description of personalities and/or occupations. The collections of personality traits and occupations are so very long for each court card that it would take a significant amount of time to go over all the possibilities with a querent and finally identify who the card represents. In addition, many of the traits are shared among several of the court cards. For example, all of the wands cards can be "warm, charismatic, and confident."

This book takes a different approach. Instead of lists of possible personalities or jobs, we will focus on the role that the court card represents. The roles are not that of king, queen, knight, or page in the traditional sense. The current ideas of what the court cards represent—a collection of complex and contradictory characters—are too unwieldy for divination purposes. Now it is time to shrink them back down to a manageable size in a way that makes sense within the context of our modern lives and our usage of the cards. The court cards' core meanings are like cookie cutters that mark a role played by a person involved in the situation. The physical appearance, personality, or occupation doesn't matter as much as what the person has to do with the situation being explored in the reading.

Journaling

Most tarot books and teachers encourage keeping a journal or a notebook of your tarot studies and practices—and I agree. A journal is a valuable companion on your tarot journeys. There are probably as many kinds of journals and as many ways to use a journal as there are tarotists. Let's take a look at a few of both.

Types of Journals

Traditional Journal

A traditional journal is any sort of bound book with blank or lined pages. They come in different sizes and qualities for every taste and every budget. You will likely find one that appeals to you and meets your need for size—or, if you are like me, you will find several and suddenly find yourself with a lovely journal collection. Some people prefer larger pages with plenty of room to write and draw. Some people like to carry their journals around in their purses or bags, so a smaller size is more practical. Journals come with lined pages for those who like to keep things neat and orderly, or unlined pages for those who like more freedom. If you like to write with markers or use paints in your journal, get one with thicker paper. Ballpoint pens and pencils work fine on thinner paper.

Three-Ring Binder

One downside of a traditional bound journal is that the pages must be kept in order. So if you want to record specific information together, you have to estimate ahead of time and reserve a certain number of pages or insert extra pages with clips or staples after the fact. With a three-ring binder, you can always add more pages where you want them. You can also, if you want, rearrange the pages, changing the organization to suit your needs if they change over time.

Computer

Many people love the tactile sensation of pen on paper. Some people couldn't care less (perhaps they just have atrocious penmanship). In any case, keeping a journal on your computer makes a lot of sense. You can organize your pages and information just as with a three-ring binder. You can add images and website addresses with ease, and access them just as easily, with a simple click. Perhaps best of all, computer journals are searchable. Imagine, after a few years of tarot study, having several notebooks and searching through them trying to find something that you just know you wrote down eight months ago but cannot remember where. The task of finding it would be much easier in an electronic file.

Blog

Blogs are free and easy. Many people take advantage of this and keep their journal—or one aspect of their journal—as a blog. Probably the biggest benefit of a blog is the opportunity for input and community. If you want to put in the effort to create a readership, the comments and insights of others can be interesting, inspiring, and thought provoking. The downside is that they are generally public places. Tarot can be a very personal and private practice, perhaps not best suited for public consumption. However, with areas that are not constricted by the need for privacy, a blog can be a fun way to track your studies. One of the most common blogging practices is the "card a day" (see page 26).

How to Use Your Journal

There are so many ways use to a journal in conjunction with tarot cards that you could write a book about it. Someone did, actually. If you enjoy journaling and want more ideas, check out Corrine Kenner's *Tarot Journaling*.

Record Your Readings

If you do nothing else with your journal, keep a record of your readings. Note the date, the spread, the deck used, and the question. Write out the interpretation, observations that stood out as particularly important, and things about the reading that confused you. If you have the means and the desire, take a photo of your reading and include it. Every once in a while, go back and review your readings. Use a different color pen and write observations about the reading, your accuracy, how you would interpret it now in hindsight, and what you've learned or realized since then, making sure to include the date of your notes. This is a wonderful way to learn and remember lessons about the cards and your life.

Card a Day

Pulling a card a day is a very popular practice among both beginners and longtime students of tarot. For the beginner, it is a great way to slowly become familiar with the cards. Either pick the cards in order or randomly. Each day, note the card selected, write out its core meaning, and include your thoughts and observations about additional meanings or messages in the card. In addition to using the card-a-day method for learning the cards, you can randomly draw a card each morning as a mini reading for the day. You can ask a specific question each time or just let the card provide good advice for the day. In the evening, record how the mini reading played out in your day. When randomly pulling a card a day, it is interesting to watch for patterns or themes, such as the same card over and over, cards of the same suit, many court cards, etc.

Free Writing

Using the tarot in free writing can work in two ways. First, you can select a card that you want to write about. As with the card-a-day technique, you can go through the cards in order or you can pick one at random. Or you can pick a card that has been on your mind or has been coming up in readings a lot, one that you have trouble understanding or that bothers you, or one that inspires you. After you pick your card, set a timer. If you are new to free writing, start with three minutes; start the timer, then start writing. Don't think about grammar or spelling. Just look at the card and write whatever comes into your mind. If nothing comes to mind, start by writing that, or try describing the card in detail. After your free-writing session, read what you have written, noticing anything that adds to your understanding of the card or piques your interest.

Another way to use free writing with your tarot cards is when you have a question or situation that is troubling you. Think about the situation and pull a card, as if you were going to do a reading. Instead of doing a regular reading, look at the card image while thinking about your question. Ask the character or characters in the card what their advice would be, and just start writing. This technique usually provides two benefits: learning some interesting advice about a problem and gaining some insight about a card. This technique is particularly entertaining if you use court cards. Ask several of the court cards for advice on the same situation and see what varied responses you'll get.

If this were a class instead of a book, this is where we'd take a little break. You've taken in a lot of information in a few short pages. You have a little tarot history under your belt. You know that a reader, a querent, a question, a spread, and a deck are needed in order to perform a reading. You learned the parts that make up a tarot deck. You have some ideas about connecting your worldview with tarot. You have begun sketching out your map. Soon it will be time to start filling in some details on the map of tarot. But first, take that little break. Stretch your legs, pet the dog, get a snack. Once you're properly refreshed, you will begin your Fool's Journey in earnest. Don't forget to bring your journal!

2: The Card Meanings

Depending on who you ask, the meaning of any card can be summed up in a single word, a sentence, a list of key words, a paragraph, or an essay. In a sense, all of those answers are correct. A single word can be used to remind the reader of an entire lifetime's learning about a card. A lengthy article can open up new and fascinating layers of a card. What if I told you that you needed to know an essay's worth of information about a card before you start reading the cards? I know that would have put me off, and I might never have begun. I don't want to give you a word or an essay, but rather I want to give you a foundation so that you can begin reading quickly and thus gain experience, build confidence, and develop your own unique interpretations and reading style.

To do that, I will focus on core meanings based on the image on each card. Dreams and symbols are how our subconscious talks to our conscious mind. Similarly, the images and symbols on the cards build a bridge between our heart and mind. There is a reason we are so drawn to the art on the tarot cards. The images move our souls and trigger our imaginations, letting us see answers and possibilities that eluded us previously.

This book is illustrated with three decks. First, the Universal Waite Tarot, which is based on the Rider-Waite-Smith Tarot (the 1909 deck that is the granddaddy of most decks designed today). This version is a very close copy but redrawn and recolored by Mary Hanson-Roberts. Second, the Legacy of the Divine Tarot, the third deck created by Ciro Marchetti, an award-winning and celebrated tarot artist, perhaps one of the best known of our day. And third, Shadowscapes, a beautiful new deck by Stephanie Pui-Mun Law with a focus on fantasy, mythology, and the natural world.

The section for each card will begin with a core meaning that applies to the card in general, followed by commentary on the three individual cards and how the images relate to the core meaning. The text will point out how the images illustrate or express the core meaning as well as how they may show subtle (or not so subtle) differences in focus. By looking at three variations in the same tradition, you'll learn how to really look at and read any card images. Once you see how easy it is to do this—how the core meanings are simply another way to say what the image conveys—you can then combine the core meaning and the image of any deck to create your own divinatory meanings that make sense to you.

The core meanings provided here have been carefully crafted and should prove to be very useful as a foundation. However, your intuition trumps everything. If you do not see the stated core meaning in the image, don't use it. Use what you see. You, after all, are the reader.

Whenever tarotists talk about the cards, it is often difficult to leave personal judgment or philosophy or advice out of the discussion. For example, in regard to the Eight of Swords, I have been known to say that although the woman is bound, blindfolded, and surrounded by swords, she can easily walk away if she wants to (her legs are unfettered). However, the image does not really show whether she can easily escape or not—it simply depicts a precarious situation. The idea that she can "easily walk away" says more about my attitude toward difficult situations than about the card image. The core meanings in this book attempt to leave behind assumptions or judgments and simply present the situation pictured in the card. The inherent goodness or badness of it is, in the end, up to you and, ultimately, the querent.

While it is very true that these core meanings are based on the images, there are a few quaint, old-fashioned fortunetelling meanings that simply delight me. Whenever these cards show up in readings, they always make me smile. They are not based on the images; indeed, I'm not really sure what they're based on besides old divination methods. But I will share these little oddities with you, which you can promptly forget or keep in your back pocket to use whenever appropriate. The Ace of Pentacles is one of my favorites; A. E. Waite wrote that this is the most fortuitous card in the deck. The Three of Wands means that good luck is on the way. The Nine of Cups was called the "wish card" and meant that your wish would be granted.

Learning core meanings for the cards will give you a good foundation upon which to build your own interpretations. As you go along, you will increase in confidence and develop your style. You will learn different techniques, some of which you will discard and some of which you will keep. Sometimes the cards will reveal a sense of humor; once, I read for a woman who wondered about pursuing a career in professional dance. I said something about if the World card shows up, we'll know she should, because the figure on that card is sometimes called "the world dancer." Wouldn't you know it ... the World was the first card we drew.

On the following pages, you will find three images of each card, the core meaning, an expanded meaning, and specific explorations of the three individual images. The cards are presented in the following order:

> **The Major Arcana, 0–XXI**
>
> **The Suit of Wands, Ace–10**
>
> **The Suit of Cups, Ace–10**
>
> **The Suit of Swords, Ace–10**
>
> **The Suit of Pentacles, Ace–10**
>
> **The Pages (Wands, Cups, Swords, Pentacles)**
>
> **The Knights (Wands, Cups, Swords, Pentacles)**
>
> **The Queens (Wands, Cups, Swords, Pentacles)**
>
> **The Kings (Wands, Cups, Swords, Pentacles)**

The court cards are quite different than the Major Arcana cards and the numbered Minor Arcana. There are four cards in each rank, and these four cards share important characteristics. Instead of repeating the same information four times over, each set of cards will be prefaced by a little introduction that tells about the qualities of each rank.

It's almost time for you to meet the cards. You can turn the page and start reading, going in the order presented here, or you can shake things up a bit. Shuffle your deck, randomly pick a card, and then read about it. Go through your deck, pick cards that appeal to you, and read about them first. Or try the opposite and start with cards that make you slightly uncomfortable or a little nervous. Personally, I'd start with the pretty ones and save the less-fun ones for a later—but then, I am the type to eat dessert first.

The Major Arcana

Although usually considered the important cards in the deck—they are, after all, the "big" secrets—the Major Arcana cards are often among the easiest to interpret. This is because they are based on archetypes, which are kind of like stock characters, like "good cops" and "bad cops" or "evil genius" or "gentle giant." Archetypes are similar to stereotypes but rather grander. They refer to mythological roles, such as the Mother, the Father, the Hero, the Wise Old Man. We can usually identify these characters when we meet them in movies or books. Even though these characters are individuals, we know something about them and about their nature because, on some level, we know and understand the archetype.

In addition to their core meanings, the Major Arcana cards bring an air of importance to a reading. They are, by name and nature, significant experiences, and their presence indicates a life lesson or experience. Like their historic role as trump cards, they can change the direction of the querent's life.

0   The Fool

While it is true that every step we take affects our future, the Fool represents a crossroads of major importance. The next step will be the start of a new journey, or phase, in our lives. As the name implies, the method for deciding this next step easily can be described as foolish by those who prefer a rational approach with lists of pros and cons. Instead of making a detailed plan, the Fool makes the decision intuitively, taking a leap of faith. There is a sense of spontaneity, but in most images the Fool carries a bag, indicating some forethought. The Fool represents moving without knowing precisely where we'll end up or how exactly we will get there.

THE FOOL.

The Fool

0

0 The Fool

The Universal Waite Fool stands under a shining sun, filling the image with optimism. He looks at the sky as if following a vision. The cliff indicates a potentially dangerous situation. The dog can be providing encouragement or a warning. This Fool is confidently following his dreams, but whether they will be ultimately realized is uncertain.

Core meaning:
The moment before the
first step is taken.

In the Legacy card, the Fool has taken at least one step. His journey is already in progress and events are already in motion, symbolized by the cards spread out before him. The hourglass with the sand at the top shows that this is indeed the start of a cycle. There is a sense of magic and surrealism. As this Fool balances on the hourglass, he appears in a precarious position, yet he seems gracefully poised, content to go with the flow.

The Shadowscapes card also shows great poise. The doves holding her ribbons represent her faith, indicating that she is confident that if she takes the leap, everything will be fine. Her trust is touching and poignant.

I   The Magician

The Magician functions by a fundamental belief:
as above, so below. This means that the higher
plane of existence is reflected in the lower plane.
It implies a connection with the Divine. If he is in
line with the Divine, he becomes a channel that
can effect change in the world. His knowledge and
understanding of the laws of the universe allow
him to use what is at hand to achieve his goals.
Combining base elements with the spirit of the
Divine allows for a result that is worth far more than
the sum of its parts. This card says that in this situation we can do the same. We have the necessary
knowledge and resources to achieve our goals.

THE MAGICIAN.

The Magician

I The Magician

In the Universal Waite card, there is a strong representation of the connection between the Divine and personal will. One hand reaches toward heaven, indicating the Divine, but it holds a wand, a symbol of will. His other hand directs the channeled energy. The white lilies represent the purity of his relationship with the Divine; the red roses, his passion or intent. The lemniscate shows that all possibilities exist within the infinite universe. The chalice, sword, and pentacle symbolize his resources.

Core meaning:
Using knowledge, resources, and will to create change in the world.

The Legacy Magician also shows a strong tie between resources, will, and the Divine. The items on his worktable are his resources, his intense focus is his will, and the electric bolt is the energy of the Divine. All these come together to create something magical and amazing. There is also a focus on knowledge, as indicated by the books in the background. His work is not intuitive; it is based on principles and ideas that he has accumulated.

The Shadowscapes Magician has a more shamanistic feel, although the principles are the same. The trinkets attached to his wings are gifts from the spirit world, representing his deep connection to the Divine. The idea of knowledge is implied, for by journeying into the realm of the Divine, he learns from spirits.

II   The High Priestess

The High Priestess guards the threshold of an initiation. An initiation provides knowledge, insight, or wisdom that cannot be taught; it can only be gained through direct experience. Because she does not share this information, this card represents something that cannot be revealed at this time. The High Priestess is connected with water, which, as author and teacher Kim Huggens points out, indicates her ability to understand the flow of the ever-changing future. The answer cannot be revealed because it is still changeable and depends on the initiate's reaction. In addition, it is only by experiencing the events to come and not knowing about them ahead of time that knowledge, insight, and wisdom may be learned.

THE HIGH PRIESTESS

The High Priestess

II The High Priestess

The Universal Waite card reflects a mystery school or secret society initiation. The High Priestess sits between two pillars, indicating a very specific and controlled point of entry. The veil decorated with pomegranates represents Persephone's journey to the underworld, or death. The water and the moon symbolize the subconscious, the unknown, and change. All these symbols together show that there is something specific that must be experienced, the details of which are unknown. The response to the experience will affect the outcome.

Core meaning:
Something that can only be understood through experience.

The Legacy High Priestess is submerged in water, symbolizing the importance of experience. The closed scroll indicates two things: this is not something that can be learned by reading or words, and it is a mystery. The pomegranate, again, speaks of Persephone's journey. The owl flying above the scene is the promise of the wisdom to be gained through this situation.

In the Shadowscapes card, the familiar pomegranate is shown, as well as the owl: the journey and the resulting wisdom. The crescent moons on her cloak show the mystery and changeable nature of the situation. The uplifted and spread arms of the Priestess represent fully embracing the experience at hand.

III   The Empress

The Empress, sometimes associated with Mother Nature, does represent nature, life, and growth. However, she represents birth and ripening, the beginning and peak of the cycle, more than death, which is the end of the cycle. The card symbolizes abundance. This not merely having enough; it is *more* than enough. This is not just nourishment; this is a feast for the senses. The Empress and her creation are lush and beautiful, with no stinginess or shabbiness. As part of nature, we also have the ability to create in this way. The act of creation and the enjoyment of abundance are linked. While it is true that we reap what we sow, and that sometimes we make poor seed choices, this card is about the good seeds. It is about creating and enjoying the good things in life.

THE EMPRESS.

The Empress

III

III The Empress

The Universal Waite Empress reigns over nature, a true empress, in complete control over her creation. Her elaborate pillows and blankets show comfort and luxury. The pomegranates show abundance, as does the wheat, which is also practical and nourishing. The stars on her crown represent time in general, and specifically the role of time and cycles in the circle of life, as well as the idea that creation takes place in the mind as well as in the world.

Core meaning:

Abundance and creation.

The Legacy Empress is more a part of her creation than in control of it. Creatures of the water, earth, and air are present, symbolizing creation in all spheres of life. Pregnant, she is blowing dandelion seeds, showing that even as she enjoys her creations, she continues to create.

The Shadowscapes card shows a scene of active and artistic creation. Although this Empress appears ethereal, she is clothed in earthy reds, greens, and golds. She has a higher focus and vision but is still grounded, showing both spiritual and physical abundance. There is a whimsical feel to the image, contrasting with the practicality in the Universal Waite card.

IV   The Emperor

Like the Empress, the Emperor is a creator, but of a different sort. The Emperor creates for the purposes of order, efficiency, prosperity, and stability. Infrastructures, systems of organization, distribution, accessibility, and storage are some examples of Emperor-like accomplishments. He surveys the entire situation and makes decisions accordingly. His position is sometimes described as one of power, but it is more specifically focused on authority and responsibility. The role of the Emperor is not to impose his will, per se, but to create order in a way that benefits the larger picture.

IV The Emperor

The Universal Waite Emperor is pictured in a desert. This symbolizes two things. First, that he makes limited resources stretch as far as possible. Second, it suggests the sun, representing solar (or male) thinking—that is, logic and rationality. His decisions are practical, not emotional. He chooses as his throne a cubelike structure, indicating the importance of a stable foundation.

Core meaning:
Creating order and stability.

The Legacy Emperor stands under the reddish yellow light of a stained glass window with the symbol of Aries in it. This, like the desert, is solar energy. It also assumes you are knowledgeable about astrology. What it means in terms of this card is "having a sense of direction and purpose." This emperor stands surrounded by circles, indicating a holistic view and working for the greater good.

In the Shadowscapes card, the Emperor's garb and headpiece symbolize the Oak King as well as Aries; again, solar energies. The circles are repeated in this image and emphasized by the Emperor's connection with the tree he stands within. His efforts are not for the advancement of his personal will. He is connected to a bigger picture, and this connection shapes his efforts.

V The Hierophant

The Hierophant is often thought of as one of the most difficult cards in the deck—not to interpret but because many people have negative responses to anything representing what they consider a restrictive or repressive organization. Its original name was the Pope, which to many people unfortunately represents oppressive or abusive religious control. The Golden Dawn changed the card to the Hierophant, which most people assume is an esoteric name for the Pope. It comes from the word *hierophany*, meaning the manifestation of the sacred. A hierophant, then, is one who teaches, who shows us how to live by our beliefs—in short, how to walk the talk. There is still the element of teaching and instruction, but there is a difference in focus. This is not about following the rules of a demanding and illogical deity. This is about how we can live our lives in a way that brings our faith or beliefs to life; it is how we manifest the sacred in this world.

THE HIEROPHANT

Faith

V

V The Hierophant

In the Universal Waite card, it is easy to focus on the formal and ritualistic nature of the card as well as the implied hierarchy. More to the point, here is the idea that the Hierophant has the formal training, personal experience, and required accountability to make him an appropriate teacher. His upraised hand has two fingers up and two down, representing the connection of higher ideals and earthly experience. His wand is topped with crosses, which symbolize the intersection between the spiritual (vertical lines) and earthly (horizontal lines).

Core meaning:
Living faith in everyday life.

The Legacy card is renamed Faith. The strong vertical pillar represents spirituality and connection to the Divine. The four figures show how connection to the Divine can be manifested in many different ways on earth. These figures suggest that through devotion, meditation, and study, we can gain understanding of our beliefs and thereby practice them in daily life.

The Shadowscapes Hierophant is an ancient tree. It represents deep roots and a long history. This tree is deeply connected to the wisdom of the earth. Because of its age, it has great experience and has witnessed many things. The light on the staff he holds shows that his faith is bright and attracts others to him. No creature is too small, no being is considered insignificant. This teacher knows that all can live according to their faith.

VI The Lovers

Almost everyone likes falling in love or being in love because of the way it makes us feel. This is a complex card about the union of opposites, communion with the Divine, and completion, but at the end of the day it is really about making a choice. Specifically, it is about making a decision that makes you feel as good, as certain, as strong (and maybe even as scared and vulnerable) as being in love makes us feel. The decision can be about any aspect of our lives. The choices can be many or few. What matters with this card is picking the option that resonates with your heart, makes you feel good about yourself, and creates the sense that all is right with the world.

THE LOVERS.

The Lovers

VI The Lovers

The Universal Waite card shows the idea of opposites mentioned earlier: man and woman, earth and fire, human and angel, obedience and temptation. There are choices to be made here. The angel represents the all-consuming love for and guidance of the Divine that dwells in our hearts. The angel is huge and the sun is shining brightly on it, indicating that this really is an obvious decision.

Core meaning:
Making a decision that
makes your heart glad.

The Legacy Lovers are just about to kiss, and the arrow is just about to pierce the apple; the decision is just about to be made. As soon as their lips touch and the apple is pierced, they will know without a doubt that they made the right choice, for their hearts led them to this moment.

In the Shadowscapes card, the Lovers have tossed aside the so-called rational decisions as they choose each other. He has let the doves take his crown, a sign of being in the ruling class; she has removed her flower wreath, indicating her peasant background. Social concerns or the expectations of others don't matter. The lilies and rose represent purity and passion, the foundation of their choice.

VII   The Chariot

This card shows the need or desire to move forward being impeded by circumstances, which may be internal or external. The difficult situation is usually based in a conflict of some sort, as shown by the two beasts attached to the chariot. The journey appears to be one of moving away from something more than toward something, as a city usually appears in the background. This indicates leaving comforts, family, and security. Therefore, the conflict can be about not wanting to leave or others not wanting us to go. And so there is a struggle, making forward movement difficult. Some believe that the charioteer exhibits mental control in order to move forward. However, if the charioteer is pictured wielding anything, it is a wand, indicating the will. In this situation, our will is our secret weapon.

THE CHARIOT.

The Chariot

VII

VII The Chariot

The Universal Waite Chariot, with its male passenger and no reins, is stalled due to two unwilling sphinxes. They represent opposing forces that won't work together, that are at cross-purposes. Sphinxes indicate riddles or mysteries, so the actual crux of the conflict is probably not revealed. The charioteer holds his wand, the sign of his will. He wears a crown of stars and in addition has a canopy of stars, representing celestial inspiration and guidance.

Core meaning:
The triumph of will in difficult circumstances.

The Legacy Chariot features a female driver holding the reins, making progress but at great peril. She leaves behind not a city but a planet, still a symbol of an existence left behind. She drives through the water using the light from her wand—that is, the clarity of her will—to guide the way. The wings represent the power of her convictions, which lend strength and speed to her journey.

The Shadowscapes Chariot shows a woman standing in her chariot; she has let the reins drop. Her steeds look back at her, as if for guidance. They seem less certain than she about the path they are on. They represent her inner conflict, her uncertainty on some level about this journey. However, she looks ahead, focusing on her goal, her destination. She lets that vision strengthen and feed her will. That alone is what urges them forward.

VIII   Strength

The lion represents the practical, assertive, or even aggressive side of our will. It is usually the ruler of us and often serves us well, but such strong approaches are not always advantageous to the situation. A quieting, controlling influence creates another kind of power altogether. This type of strength can be respected without being feared. The gentle open hand transfers peace, soothing the situation. Interestingly, this card almost always features a female figure calming the beast, representing feminine energy. She usually touches his head—that is, she calms his thoughts and probably guides them in another direction, thereby taking control and redirecting the situation.

VIII Strength

The Universal Waite Strength card shows the connection between gentleness and the flow of divine power by picturing a lemniscate over the woman's head. Her white gown indicates the purity of her intention. The lion's mouth is the center of the image, a focal point. He is being loud and dangerous. She says, "Hush now, be quiet, be calm."

Core meaning:
Calm control that soothes
the situation.

The Legacy card also shows a connection with divine power. The woman touches the animals on their heads, which light up. Their crown chakras have been activated, allowing them connection with divinity. Her influence allows them to know a kind of peace and power they weren't aware of before.

In the Shadowscapes card, different types of strength are shown by the presence of the lion and of the cats. The woman touches the lion's head, quieting his mind. She is also touching his mouth, helping control his destructive inclinations. The swan on the lion's back reminds us that this kind of strength is transformative both to those who experience it and to situations, turning a potentially ugly one into something more pleasant.

IX   The Hermit

Most Hermit cards are in shades of blue, featuring a mysterious cloaked figure. The most predominant visual aspect is the light from the lantern. That light is the focus of this card; it represents our own spark of divinity. The light of that spark is what should guide our paths. This card represents no longer listening to others; even, in this situation, removing ourselves from their influence. It is our own truth that should lead us. The Hermit is sometimes seen as a teacher or a guide. In reality, this card is about an act of self-discovery. Having a clear, bright light—that knowing that guides our steps—can attract others who want to follow or learn. This is not a role the Hermit seeks; it is more the purview of the Hierophant, who is called to teach. Instead, the Hermit, by definition, is solitary; his life is an example, but his journey is not a public classroom.

THE HERMIT.

The Hermit

IX

IX The Hermit

The Universal Waite Hermit is so archetypal in appearance that he is almost a caricature. He is a wise old man using his truth to light his path. His staff, which is a very large wand, represents his will, which has grown strong over the years and supports him on his journey.

Core meaning:
Retreating from distractions to determine your own truth.

The Legacy card shows a man with a careworn face, tall mountains, and deep valleys. His journey has not been an easy one. His truths were hard won. A brightly glowing crystal tops his wand, symbolizing the union and complete integration of his truth and his will.

In the Shadowscapes card, the Hermit has ascended great spiritual heights and is nose to nose with the Divine. His truth and universal truth are about to become one. He carries no staff at all, indicating that he has no will separate from that of his truth.

X   The Wheel of Fortune

The only constant is change. We can say that whatever comes up must go down. We can assume that
the Wheel turns in a slow, natural progression,
allowing us to experience each side in turn. But that
would be a mistake. The Wheel doesn't always just
turn—sometimes it is spun. And when it is, where
will it stop? No one knows. This card does not represent the slow, expected turning, for why would
something natural and expected need to be foretold?
This card lets us know that the Wheel is about to be
spun, meaning things may be up in the air for a bit.

WHEEL of FORTUNE.

The Wheel

X

X The Wheel

In the Universal Waite Wheel, a sphinx sits at the top, representing mystery, riddles, and the unpredictable spinning of the Wheel and the role of fate. The figures in the four corners represent the four fixed signs of the zodiac. It is a philosophical observation that the foundations of the world actually stay constant, and it is we who are the Wheel and doing the actual changing.

Core meaning:
Random change is at hand.

The Legacy Wheel has a mechanistic look to it. Along with the planets and stars, this says to us that this is not personal, it just happens sometimes.

The Shadowscapes Wheel shows the idea of change in the crumbling background wall, slow but inexorable. The intricate window represents the connectedness of all things. This is also a philosophic image: be comforted, do not fear change; it is all just part of a bigger picture.

XI Justice

Unlike the Wheel of Fortune, Justice's consequences are not random. This is the card of reaping what you've sown, for good or ill—a time of karmic accounting, so to speak. This is not necessarily a bad card. It is not saying that you did anything wrong. Like the double-edged sword (representing law) that Justice wields, it can go either way. And which-ever way it goes, Justice will use her other favorite tool, the scales, to matter-of-factly measure out the results. Like the High Priestess, Justice sits between two pillars, representing a threshold. The meaning of the card isn't simply that "whatever you receive, you earned." It is also a gift of entry to another realm of understanding. It teaches us how the uni-verse works, so we can function better within it.

XI Justice

The Universal Waite Justice sits before a veil that reminds us that her intricate logic and infallible understanding of the facts are far beyond our mere human comprehension. Her crown indicates her authority. The sword and scales symbolize the law and payment due. Justice is not blindfolded; she clearly sees all aspects of the matter and can ascertain the truth.

Core meaning:
The consequences of your actions are at hand.

The Legacy Justice card emphasizes the two aspects of Justice by showing two figures instead of one: the interpretation of the law and the payment required in the face of that interpretation. These figures are shown blindfolded as a sign of impartiality, or seeing beyond the surface into the truth of a matter. Together, these facets of justice create perfect and natural balance in the world.

The Shadowscapes card shows a popular version of Justice: the Egyptian goddess Ma'at. When a person dies, Ma'at weighs their heart against a feather. If they balance—that is, if the heart is light—the person goes on to the afterlife. If not, the heart is eaten by a demon.

XII · The Hanged Man

Early decks did not show the serene image we find today. Those first decks depicted the Hanged Man as a traitor. Tarot evolved, and now the symbol has taken on a different meaning. Modern images show a quiet, accepting figure, sometimes with a holy glow or tranquil expression. Many people think of this card as sacrifice, but that is not quite it. This card is a type of surrender that is willing. There is no flailing or fighting, no struggle or stress; instead, it is a period of letting go, of releasing, of doing nothing. Time is suspended, and we must simply observe, reflect, wait, and accept.

THE HANGED MAN.

The Hanging Man

XII

XII The Hanged Man

The Universal Waite card shows a halo around the Hanged Man's head, representing that this experience of observing and reflecting leads to spiritual understanding. He hangs from a living tree, symbolizing that this situation connects him to divine wisdom and is also rooted to earth and will have practical applications.

Core meaning:
Willing surrender to an experience or situation.

The Legacy image shows the Hanged Man gracefully suspended between sky and water. The hourglass lying on its side echoes this idea: time has, for now, stopped. The mask falls from his face. He has no persona to maintain and no roles to play. He drops coins, symbolizing his willing release from his attachment to the things of the world—at least for now.

The Shadowscapes card also eliminates the idea of hanging. This Hanged Man swings from a branch, allowing the tree to wrap around him as he seeks to become one with it. He wants to absorb and embody its wisdom and strength. The ankh hanging from the tree's upper branch is an Egyptian symbol for life, illustrating that, at this time, his life is suspended.

XIII   Death

This card rarely means physical death. Most modern interpretations of the Death card focus on transformations and new beginnings. However, before that comes the ending of something. It is this ending that people fear, and we try to gloss over it by talking about the new and presumably better time to come. That may all be so, but we show a lack of courage and commitment to truth when we minimize the experience of death. People experiencing the Death card both need and have a right to their grief and sense of loss. Hope is almost always present in most versions of the Death card, sometimes taking the form of a sunrise, a white rose, or a phoenix. But the images also present the dark side of death, with skulls, reapers, and engulfing flames. It is important not to skip the hard part and jump directly to the potential shiny new future.

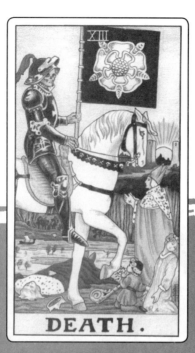

DEATH.

XIII Death

The Universal Waite card shows different approaches to death: the fainting king, pleading bishop, swooning maiden, innocent child. Along with the promise of a new day, Death comes riding into our lives. The end is inevitable; the new beginning is full of promise. The question in this card is how we greet death.

Core meaning:
An ending that makes transformation possible.

The Legacy card shows the moment between death and transformation. The card almost reeks of decay and pain. Out of the decomposing remains, a white rose grows. At this point, the bloom is hardly visible.

In the Shadowscapes card, the phoenix—a mythical bird that rises from the ashes of its own death to be born anew—is a popular symbol for modern versions of the Death card. It beautifully conveys the idea of a clear ending leading to a promising future. Sumac is on the branch with the phoenix. In Victorian times, sumac conveyed the message that "I shall survive this change."

XIV   Temperance

Temperance is usually interpreted as balance or moderation. That is a good start, but it's overly simplistic. Temperance is not about balance in terms of "equal parts"; instead, it has a more alchemical approach. This is about the right combination of parts, which may or may not be equal. For example, the idea of a balanced life usually means making room in our daily lives for work, rest, and play. However, there are times when such a moderate balance is not the best approach. Training for a marathon, studying for an exam, or planning a party or large event, for example, may call for more concentrated focus, for more time and attention. This card is about the right parts coming together in a kind of magical way to create something wonderful. Like alchemy, it is the transmutation of lead into gold.

TEMPERANCE.

Temperance

XIV

XIV Temperance

The Universal Waite card shows the angel with one foot on land and one in the water. The perfect balance allows magic to happen: the water is flowing between the cups in a way that defies gravity. The angel's halo represents serenity, and the red wings are power; both are in exquisite balance.

Core meaning:
The right thing at the right time in the right place.

The Legacy card represents a balance of apparent contradictions: the angel is suspended in air yet stationary, and she holds fire and water. Blending opposites in perfectly equal parts would negate both. This angel can mix them to create something that is neither.

The Shadowscapes card illustrates the blending of opposites: scales and feathers, fire and water. Her creation resembles a yin/yang symbol. Everything holds the seed of its opposite.

XV   The Devil

In many decks, the Devil is a parody of the Hierophant and the Lovers. This tells us two very important
things. First, because it is parody, it can seem correct
and appropriate—at first glance. As a parody, it is
also attractive (parodies are usually funny, clever,
or witty). Second, the Hierophant and the Lovers
represent walking according to our beliefs and making choices that make our hearts happy. The Devil,
then, represents living in a way that is contrary to our
beliefs and in a way that saddens our souls. This card
represents what is wrong for us in a situation. It is
often interpreted as bondage or addiction. The idea
of being bound or controlled is apt, as the Devil (however it manifests) holds us back; we make no forward
progress on our path, either spiritual or mundane.

The Universal Waite card presents a stereotypical Christian devil image. The devil figure represents the behavior or situation that holds us in bondage. The male and female characters with tails and horns make a mockery of what it means to be human. The chains appear loose enough that escape would be simply a matter of choice, but the figures make no progress.

Core meaning:
A choice, action, or situation contrary to your best interest.

The Legacy card highlights the attractiveness and seductiveness of temptation. As in the Hanged Man card, the hourglass is on its side, representing time standing still and the lack of progress. Unlike the peaceful Hanged Man, though, this figure is tortured.

The Shadowscapes card focuses on the fragility of bondage: the thread binding her is thin, and besides, the key is right above. It also shows the completeness of the bondage: she is captured in a circle (a circle is a sign of completeness). Her heart, in the grasp of the dancing devil above her, has been stolen so that she no longer has a moral compass.

XVI   The Tower

Sometimes we build something, such as a home, career, relationship, or belief system. We care for it, love it, and come to depend on it. Then, out of the blue, something occurs that changes everything. Our cherished creation is knocked down, utterly destroyed, and we are surrounded by shambles. The Tower represents this experience—and a little more. It is not merely destruction for destruction's sake; it is a breakdown that allows for a break-through. It releases us from what no longer serves our best interest. It takes away what is no longer good or sound. The Tower destroys something as we know it, thereby providing the raw material and experience to re-create something new.

THE TOWER.

XVI The Tower

The Universal Waite Tower—although on fire and hit by lightning—looks like it might survive. The human figures falling from it, on the other hand, look like they are in for a rough landing. In this card, the focus is on the effect this experience will have on the person or people experiencing it, as well as on the structure itself.

Core meaning:
An unexpected event that changes everything.

The Legacy Tower is a beautiful and delicate creation. It also appears to have been precariously built, a subtle built-in warning about the importance of having a good foundation. If any one of those legs is hit, the whole thing collapses.

The Shadowscapes Tower is a complex and unique tree. The idea of nature destroying itself is particularly difficult to accept, but it does happen. The focus of this card is on the seemingly random and inexplicable nature of the event.

XVII   The Star

Stars have played roles both mythic and mundane in the lives of humans. We like to wish upon a star. Looking at the stars gives us perspective. Stars are used for navigation. The constellations tell stories; we use them to find understanding, direction, and hope. Their gentle yet brilliant light gives comforting hope in times of darkness. They are not illusionary like the moon nor overwhelming like the sun. They are soft, gentle, and yet amazingly powerful. This card brings refreshment and cleansing after trouble. It promises restored faith and renewed purpose.

THE STAR.

The Star

XVII

XVII The Star

The Universal Waite Star is naked, symbolizing being at our most vulnerable. She pours water from the twin pitchers of faith and trust, showing that at this time we need to put our faith and trust in the universal flow of the Divine.

Core meaning:

Guidance, serenity, and hope.

The Legacy Star dances above a scene of devastation. She gives us what we need in order to leave the wreckage behind—not in despair, but in hope.

In the Shadowscapes card, the Star rises above troubled waters. She does not drown but walks gently amongst fish flourishing out of water, her healing flowing behind her. She says that we also will not drown and that her power will help us believe what might seem unbelievable.

XVIII   The Moon

The Moon is a complex and uncertain card. Modern tarotists are hesitant to read it as strictly negative, because of its association with feminine energy and the goddess. The moon appears to change in the sky each night, waxing and waning through its cycles, indicating a situation that is changing. What might be true today may not be true tomorrow. The moon reflects light, but it is shadowy and conceals as much as it reveals. Things that seem lovely in the moonlight may be monsters by the light of day, and vice versa. The moon heightens the gifts of intuition and creativity. It calls forth fears. It creates delusions. This card says, "Be careful; things are not necessarily as they seem."

The **Universal Waite Moon** shines over a crayfish, representing deep fears, and a wolf, representing animalistic responses. A domesticated dog will bay like a wild creature under the influence of the moon. The path is a reminder to not be distracted or dismayed but to stick to our route. The towers represent a threshold (as in the High Priestess and Justice). If we face our fears successfully, we will enter a new aspect of our journey.

Core meaning:
A situation of flux and uncertainty, either fraught with deception or revealing important truths.

The **Legacy Moon card** includes a crab, representing fear, a woman, representing beauty, and a pair of ibises, representing truth. Of this card, Ruth Ann and Wald Amberstone have written, "the mythical becomes real and the real becomes inexplicably beautiful." This version focuses on the attractive and hypnotic nature of the moon.

The **Shadowscapes card** includes mushrooms, indicating the hallucinogenic property of the moon. The figure holds a mask, representing deception, in one hand, and her heart in the other. She is facing the mask, symbolizing the ease with which we can turn to what is untrue and miss the voice of our hearts.

XIX   The Sun

Unlike the Moon, this card is straightforward. Like a perfect sunny day, it is positive, happy, and joyful. What was in the darkness is now revealed. We can see clearly, and what we see pleases us. Unlike the Tower, which brings a clarity that changes everything, the Sun brings a clarity that says all is right with the world. The Sun is the quintessential feeling of being present in a particularly good moment: everything is exactly as it should be.

THE SUN .

The Sun

XIX

XIX The Sun

The Universal Waite card shows a child riding a white horse, symbolizing an innocent and childlike acceptance of joy. The sunflowers indicate optimism.

Core meaning:

Clarity that brings joy.

The Legacy card shows less overt joy. The figure stands before his vision of the universe. He finally understands the purpose of all things in the universe and has them lined up properly. Order reigns, and with it comes confidence and stability.

The Shadowscapes card shows a joyous scene. The man is gazing upon something that we cannot see. His gesture indicates that he has witnessed the greatness of the universe. His feelings include reverence and humbleness as well as joy.

XX   Judgement

This card could benefit from a new title. Too many of us see it and think that it means we are being judged—that meaning, though, belongs to the Justice card. This card is about hearing a call and answering it. The image shows the dead, lifeless, and stagnant people being awoken; by responding to the call, they find renewed life. This card is also associated with forgiveness. If we are called upon to forgive and we do, we are renewed and freed. If we do not and instead decide to foster a grudge, we remain as we were, trapped in anger or hurt. So, Judgement can mean a call of any sort. Whether or not we act on the call determines the ultimate outcome.

JUDGEMENT.

Judgement

XX

XX Judgement

The Universal Waite card shows a stereotypical Judgment Day scene. The dead, in their caskets, represent the limiting boxes we find ourselves in—and need, sometimes, to be called from. The figures are welcoming the call, glad to be awakened from their lifeless states.

Core meaning:
Hearing and heeding a call.

The Legacy card is even more emotionally evocative. The angel appears to be longing for the answer, more passionate in its plea. The rising figures answer the call with beatified grace. It is easy to imagine they were not dead but in an agony worse than death.

In the Shadowscapes Judgement, the focus is on the call itself, with the rising being almost hidden in the flow of her garment. It implies that by following the call of the Divine, we will find ourselves in a transformative universal flow.

XXI   The World

The World, a glorious card that we are always happy to get, has something in common with the Death card, one most of us prefer not to see. It is, like Death, an ending. However, death is usually something that happens; the World is something we achieve. The World indicates a successful outcome to the situation or an undertaking. This event provides not just the usual happy benefits—pride, a sense of accomplishment, recognition, rewards—but also something more. With this success comes an understanding of connection between endings and beginnings, a sense of the proper flow of the universe. At this moment, everything has clicked into place. We understand ourselves and our place in the world. The World also has much in common with the Fool, for it too marks a new beginning.

THE WORLD.

The World

XXI

XXI The World

The Universal Waite World is very bold in its statement of success, for it depicts a huge laurel wreath. The actual success is dominant, but the idea of universal connection is also present in the same four fixed signs of the zodiac that are in the Wheel of Fortune and red ribbons on the wreath that form lemniscates.

Core meaning:

Successful completion.

The Legacy World shows the completion of a journey with an hourglass showing all the sand in the bottom half. The zodiac symbols circling the figure represent an understanding of universal flow. The figure has removed its mask, representing that this has also been a journey of self-discovery.

The Shadowscapes card also shows the acquisition of self-knowledge. Her crown represents enlightenment; her belt is, according to the artist, the girdle of truth. The idea of "as above, so below" is another aspect of universal flow; this figure has reached that understanding. Her glowing globe mirrors the moon.

The Minor Arcana

There are more than twice as many Minor Arcana cards (if you include the court cards) as there are Major Arcana cards. This is because most of our lives are made up of everyday life situations, not milestones. The moments pictured here may not be life altering, but as they are what fill the majority of our days, they are still important. You are apt to see all your pleasures, disappointments, conflicts, joys, achievements, family, friends, and colleagues in these images—the things and people that make up your real life.

Ace of Wands

Like all of the aces, the Ace of Wands is a gift or unexpected opportunity. The aces indicate a moment in time filled with fortuitous possibility. The power of the aces shows up in our lives when circumstances are just right for action. Acting quickly is the best way to take advantage of the aces, as these moments do not last long. If we don't take advantage of the opportunity, it passes us by. Aces are also seeds of great promise. Whatever is planted or initiated at this time has the potential for success.

Because this is a wands card, it contains the fiery energy of all the wands. This energy is manifested in several ways: passion, inspiration, courage, will, action, optimism. It is particularly suited for career-related activities and projects or plans of any sort. The Ace of Wands is the universe giving us a "thumb's up" sign. It tells us to "just do it"—act on that idea or accept that challenge.

ACE of WANDS.

Wands

Ace

Ace of Wands

In the Universal Waite card, the image of the hand emerging from the cloud highlights the idea of a gift being given. The wand is alive, showing the potential for growth, the possibilities inherent in the gift. The cloud underlines the idea of a temporary moment: wait too long, and the circumstances will change.

Core meaning:
An opportunity to take action.

In the Legacy card, the wand hovers above a pit of fire and earth. The mundane element of earth coupled with the energy of fire can yield amazing results. The wand is topped with jewels, showing the transformative potential.

In the Shadowscapes card, the foxes represent the importance of using your wit and cleverness to make the most of the opportunity at hand. The setting (or perhaps rising) of the sun hints at the transitory nature of this opportunity.

Two of Wands

The Two of Wands indicates balance between energy and vision. To accomplish something, we need the necessary energy. This card says that it is time to gather or generate that energy. An abundance of energy without direction doesn't accomplish much, though. In order to direct that energy, we need a vision. It is time to identify intentions, to see the goal very clearly. In many ways, this is the card of creative visualization. The act of focusing on the desired outcome is also an act of manifestation.

Two of Wands

The Universal Waite card highlights the importance of energy coupled with vision by showing it three times. The man is holding the world (his vision) and a wand (energy); he has these well in hand and in his control. There is also a wand nearby and he is gazing out to sea, indicating that he continues to gather energy and to refine and expand his vision. He steadies his wand atop a cube decorated with white lilies and red roses, symbols of purity of intention (vision) and passion (energy), respectively.

Core meaning:
Gathering energy while
refining your vision.

In the Legacy card, the red- and purple-tipped wand on the left shows passion, and the bluish white wand on the right is purity. By combining these appropriately, we find the key to unlock the box and achieve our desires. But in this card, there are two boxes. The designer of this deck suggests another level of meaning, saying that the red wand also shows materialism and the white wand, spirituality. The ratio of materialism and spirituality, then, also determines the final nature of the outcome.

The Shadowscapes card brings another characteristic of the wands to this card. The lion shows that courage must be present to utilize the power generated by the twin aspects of energy and vision.

Three of Wands

The idea of active waiting may sound like a contradiction in terms; however, it has much in common with the practice of active listening. In active listening, the listener is being particularly receptive, taking in everything the speaker is saying, how it is being said, body language, etc. Receptivity is often thought of as passive, but it isn't always. In baseball or in football, an outfielder or wide receiver receives the ball—but they don't just stand there waiting for it to come to them. They are watching the action, focusing on the ball, and preparing themselves to catch the ball. They are also poised with a plan for what they will do after they get the ball.

In the Two of Wands, there is a focus on gathering and releasing energy toward a vision. The Three of Wands is the time between the energy being released and the goal being realized. It is a time of strong belief in the desired outcome, watching for it, doing what is possible to ease its progress, and being ready to act once it arrives.

Three of Wands

In the Universal Waite card, the figure is waiting for his ship to come in. The assumption is that it is certainly on its way, so he'd best be on the lookout for it.

Core meaning:
Active waiting.

In the Legacy card, the goal is in sight, highlighting the importance of active waiting. Ruth Ann and Wald Amberstone wrote of this particular card that "your faith will create the lights that will lead your vision home." This is highlighted by the glowing jewels at the top of the wands.

In the Shadowscapes card, we see the idea of active waiting taken a little further to active faith. We get the sense that as this figure takes a step out onto air, the bridge appears beneath her feet. She is not just actively waiting; she is acting as if what she wants is already there.

Four of Wands

In the Four of Wands, we see the final result of a plan. What started out as a seed or small but confident step (think of the Ace of Wands) has reached a successful completion. The formal education is over, the harvest is in, the event came off without a hitch, or the job promotion was granted—the work is done, and now it is time to celebrate.

Four of Wands

The Universal Waite card shows the social aspect of the celebration, with many people involved—and with more on the way, as the women raise their bouquets in greeting. The bower made of wands and the flower garland give the sense of temporariness. This is a celebration and not a permanent way of life. Have fun, and enjoy the moment.

Core meaning:
Celebrating the culmination of events or the manifestation of a goal.

The Legacy card shows that such celebrations help connect everyone involved to a higher source, as shown by the beams of light energizing each of the wands. This connection allows an oasis to form under the wands. This refreshing energy can be taken with us even after the celebration is over, to help us through less pleasant times. Knowing that a celebration or holiday is in the future can make hard times more bearable. But a rainbow, a symbol of hope, is fleeting, reminding us of the temporary nature of celebrations.

The Shadowscapes card is filled with joyous springlike energy. The roses and falling rose petals bring to mind a wedding, a beautiful culmination of a relationship. The many creatures allude to the social aspect of such celebrations. The leaping horned creatures and fairies in flight echo the idea that this is but a moment in time, not a permanent state.

Five of Wands

The intensity of conflict can range from competition, which is usually viewed as positive, to aggressive anger, which is generally considered negative. Conflict can arise in many different situations. It can occur in a committee meeting, in the middle of a crisis, or between family members or friends planning a holiday or event. At its base, conflict is people finding their wills or desires being thwarted by other people's wills or desires. What this person wants is not what the other person wants; conflict is just that. But it often generates hurtful, destructive, and angry energy that is difficult to manage and gets in the way of useful solutions.

Five of Wands

The Universal Waite card shows many people involved, indicating a group situation. They all seem almost playful at the moment, indicating more of a contest, or competition, rather than a fight.

Core meaning:
Conflict.

In the Legacy card, there is only one character shown five times. Dragons can be seen in the background. This card is less about a group situation and more about inner conflict—about fighting one's inner dragons.

The Shadowscapes card also shows one person. It lacks the feeling of anger or really any negative emotions. Instead, there is a focus on the excitement and adrenaline felt when facing and overcoming obstacles.

Six of Wands

Unlike the communal celebration in the Four of Wands, this card focuses on the recognition and celebration of the accomplishment of a single person. It is a happy and public occasion for the one being recognized. Victory of some sort is inferred. The person is the center of attention and the focus of the limelight. Public accolades are generally considered positive events. Victories and accomplishments bring satisfaction in and of themselves, but being honored by others definitely adds to the happiness. There is also a certain joy felt by those doing the honoring—pride in the achievement of a friend, gratefulness for what was accomplished, or even a sense of relief in the presence of reliable leadership.

Six of Wands

The Universal Waite card shows the public in the background. They set the stage, but it is the figure on horseback that is the focus. He wears and carries laurel wreaths, symbols of honor. The audience lifts their wands as if in unity with the hero. This card conveys the feeling that although one person is being honored, everyone benefits in some way.

Core meaning:
Recognition of achievement.

The Legacy card lacks the community feeling—at least regarding other people. Instead, the community aspect is represented by an arch erected in the hero's honor. It looks as though it should be a great and glorious event; although colorful and dramatic, there is a sense of loneliness.

The card from Shadowscapes also shows a single person. He is clearly proud of his achievement, holding aloft his laurel wreath and standing on a sculpture of a lion, an elephant, and a snail. There is a sense of wanting all present—if, indeed, *anyone* is present—to bow down before him.

Seven of Wands

Being in a defensive position implies two things: having something to defend and being attacked. Whether the "something to defend" is worth defending, whether the attack is really a true attack, or whether the outcome will be favorable all depends on the situation—or, in the case of a reading, on the other cards in the spread or the details of the card from the deck being used. Whatever the details, feeling defensive usually is not a pleasant or enjoyable experience. It is easy to feel judged, abused, or unjustly treated. However, there are those who do enjoy the opportunity to use their courage and determination in this manner.

Seven of Wands

The Universal Waite card shows a figure defending himself from higher ground, usually considered a favorable position. He seems to be well prepared. Although outnumbered, it looks as though he could prevail.

Core meaning:
Defensiveness.

In the Legacy card, a figure is just entering through a doorway, and a number of wands, or adversaries, are in her path. She faces the necessary challenge of defending her right to continue on her chosen way. The light at the top of her wand indicates the importance of being aligned with what she believes to be right. From this, she gains the will to face these obstacles.

The Shadowscapes card shows a mother fox defending her young against a deadly attacker. The focus is on having something worth fighting for; this sense of purpose provides the courage and will to prevail. Here, the fight evokes a more emotional reaction. It is more raw—more "life and death"—than the other two cards.

Eight of Wands

Sometimes events move very quickly, and this card represents those moments. During these periods of our lives, our control varies. Things may be in perfect order, or so we think, but once set in motion, they can be affected by outside influences. In addition, we may assume a plan will have a certain outcome, but unforeseen consequences can arise. In the Eight of Wands, swift action is the only guarantee. It can upset the best-laid plans. It can beneficially facilitate everything. It can sweep us off our feet and carry us in another direction entirely.

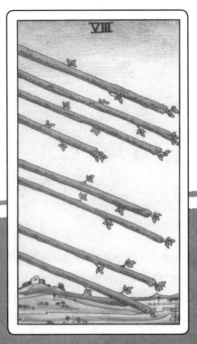

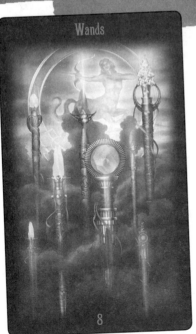

Eight of Wands

The Universal Waite card shows events already in motion heading toward their ultimate conclusion. In this card, the focus is on the events, their motion, and our lack of further control in the situation.

Core meaning:
Swift movement.

The Legacy card takes a slightly different view. The wands are all set in place. Everything appears to be in order. The archer in the background represents the constellation Sagittarius and an unexpected, swift energy. How that incoming energy will affect the situation is unknown.

The Shadowscapes card shows even less certainty. The vagaries of the wind will take the seeds of her intent where they will. And, even then, more uncertainty … will they fall in good soil, will they find enough water, will sunlight reach them? With this card, there is far less illusion of control and even more likelihood of being carried in some unknown direction.

Nine of Wands

While this card doesn't depict the most pleasant of experiences, it does depict something powerful, beautiful, and honorable. In this card, we find the element of wands, fire, at its best, representing the strength of the human spirit. This is a card of having been tried by fire and made better for it. Reliance, strength, patience, vigilance, courage, and wisdom are hard-won virtues. But there is also a certain sadness to the card, an expectation of a renewed attack. The Nine of Wands indicates that the person in question has been through a hard time, has survived, and has become stronger. It also says that the person is expecting and ready for another challenge. Whether or not that challenge will actually materialize is not indicated.

Nine of Wands

In the Universal Waite card, the wounded figure has regrouped. He watches the horizon and waits for what is to come without illusions and with the resolve to face it as best he can. The focus of this card is quiet, patient readiness and total self-reliance.

Core meaning:
Preparing for the next challenge.

The Legacy card shows a powerful figure kneeling in the light of the moon and the light of wands beside him. The tip of the wand he holds glows red, representing the passion and strength of his will. And yet, for all his physical strength and intensity of will, the act of humbleness shows yet an even greater strength. His preparation for what is to come has less to do with watching than keeping himself in readiness through his devotions.

In the Shadowscapes card, a warrior and his troops wait and watch. Filled with resolve, their wounds healed but not forgotten, they form a perfect picture of courage and vigilance.

Ten of Wands

Burdens come in many forms: responsibilities, the expectations of others, necessities. They may be taken on voluntarily or thrust upon us. They may feel heavy all the time or sometimes have no weight whatsoever. Whether life-consuming or a minor inconvenience—whether constant, intermittent, or temporary—the main point about a burden is that it is something we wish we didn't have to do or carry. In and of itself, this card doesn't tell us whether we should lay down the burden, find a better way to carry it, or just keep carrying it. It simply shows that it exists.

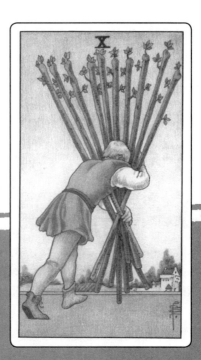

Ten of Wands

The Universal Waite card shows a figure carrying a great unwieldy load while walking toward a goal. This load makes the journey harder but not impossible. The implication here is that the goals of getting to the house and carrying the wands can both be achieved. One can hardly resist asking, though, might there not be a better way to carry the wands?

Core meaning:
Carrying a large burden
or many burdens.

In the Legacy card, we see a figure with a cumbersome burden that is seriously impeding his progress. Unlike the Universal Waite card, this card seems to imply that a choice will have to be made.

In the Shadowscapes card, the burden seems heavier and more ominous than in the other cards. This tree being has the responsibility for so much. The world she carries on her back impedes the sunlight, symbolically sapping her energy. Her well-being is at stake.

Ace of Cups

Like all of the aces, the Ace of Cups is a gift or unexpected opportunity. The aces indicate a moment in time filled with fortuitous possibility. The power of the aces shows up in our lives when circumstances are just right for action. Acting quickly is the best way to take advantage of the aces, as these moments do not last long. If we don't take advantage of the opportunity, it passes us by. Aces are also seeds of great promise. Whatever is planted or initiated at this time has the potential for success.

Because this is a cups card, it contains the watery energy of all the cups. This energy is manifested in several ways: love, affection, healing, intuition, and creativity. It is particularly suited for relationships, artistic endeavors, and spiritual journeys. The Ace of Cups invites us to drink deeply and be fulfilled—or, better yet, just jump right in.

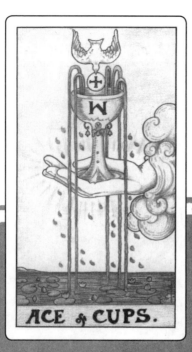

ACE of CUPS.

Cups

Ace

Ace of Cups

In the Universal Waite card, the proffered chalice has a distinctively Catholic look to it. This is not surprising, as Waite came from a Christian background. Rather than focus on the engulfing and sometimes overwhelming experience of human emotions, this card presents divine love, healing, and grace.

Core meaning:
An opportunity for an emotional experience or growth.

The Legacy card shows a fully submerged cup. It appears to be an organic part of this dark and mysterious world but clearly retains its individuality. This suggests diving into the ocean but not losing yourself completely. The illumination comes through the water itself, another reminder that emotions become filters and affect the way we see things—not that an emotional view is bad or wrong; just be aware that it may be different.

The chalice in the Shadowscapes card floats on top of the water. It is our connection to the vast world of emotions and the collective unconscious. It invites us to partake but reminds us that every movement in the world—every drop, no matter how small—causes ripples.

Two of Cups

The Two of Cups is a welcome card for those interested in a new relationship, for it is about that exciting time when people first meet and acknowledge
their attraction. This is not only romantic, for deep
emotional connections occur between friends, teachers and students, or collaborators. It may even mean
a strong emotional attraction to something rather
than someone, such as a new interest or hobby, or a
possible course of study, particularly one that is artistic or intuitive in nature. The card doesn't necessarily
say if the connection will be long lasting or whether
it will be entirely good; it simply says that it exists.

Two of Cups

The Universal Waite card focuses on the powerful effects of a relationship based on such an emotional connection. The behavior of the two figures is very formal and dignified. If they touch at all, it is possible their fingertips brush as his hand reaches toward her cup. From their union healing arises, symbolized by the caduceus. In addition, this partnership elevates our base animal tendencies, as shown by the lion with wings.

Core meaning:
Deep emotional connection or attraction.

The Legacy card shows a more complex picture of new love. There is the total immersion in the experience, which most people desire, but it can be overwhelming. The crab under the water, like the crayfish in the Moon card, represents deep fears. The hands rising from the water twine and cross and are joined by a chain, showing how quickly they've become connected. In the glasses we see one of the strongest allures of being in love: having our best selves reflected back at us in the eyes of another.

The Shadowscapes card presents the intimacy and wonder of the moment. These two also twine together; indeed, it seems as if soon they will be indistinguishable from one another. As is the case with many new lovers, they have eyes only for each other. The cup balancing on the edge of the tree being's root is the only slightly precarious piece in this puzzle. What is in that cup that is being so neglected, and will it matter if it tips over?

Three of Cups

Getting together with friends or family is often an enjoyable experience. Sometimes there are moments that surpass that pleasant feeling—joy and happiness, often combined with laughter that rises from deep within, fills your entire being and permeates everyone present. Usually there is nothing particularly noteworthy or perhaps even memorable happening. What is remembered is the general feeling of goodwill, contentment, and the sense that everything is right with the world … even if only for that moment. It is usually a shared experience, resulting from the synergy of the group, but it can be felt when alone, when happiness fills the heart for no apparent reason. This card represents those moments or that feeling.

Three of Cups

The Universal Waite card features abundance and simple pleasures, with its pumpkin and grapes. It looks like a feast or a party. The three women with their uplifted cups represent the social aspect and mutual affection. Fun, frivolity, and overflowing happiness abound.

Core meaning:
A spontaneous, unexpected joy or pleasure.

The Legacy card hints at the social aspect with the various instruments, but the main focus is on the experience of the individual. The scarf across her eyes, as well as the water splashing around her, highlights the feeling of experiencing everything through the lens of joyful emotion. When filled with such delight, everything seems better.

The Shadowscapes card shows the figures surrounded by a bubble. The bubble creates a sacred space filled with their emotions. It protects them, at least for the moment, from outside influences. Within its realm, they are very much in the moment and happily relishing it. The bubble highlights the idea of spontaneity and temporariness.

Four of Cups

Dissatisfaction with present circumstances is a common-enough experience. Being dissatisfied can bring about positive results by encouraging us to imagine things differently, which can lead to improvements, progress, and innovations. However, the result can be much more negative if it draws us into boredom, for example, or criticalness or apathy. The Four of Cups does not necessarily represent a specific response; it is more about the feeling of being dissatisfied.

Cups

4

Four of Cups

The Universal Waite card shows a man who is unhappy with the options set in front of him in the form of cups. He has either lost interest in the ideal—represented by the hand presenting a cup, reminiscent of the gift given in the Ace of Cups—or he has not yet seen it. In this image, it is not completely clear whether he will give in to apathy or if he will see a new possibility.

Core meaning:
Dissatisfaction with reality.

The Legacy card shows a man who is dissatisfied with the reality that surrounds him. None of the goblets on the ground completely please him. Instead of turning away and pouting, he imagines his ideal goblet. By visualizing it, he is one step closer to creating it, although at this point it still is not guaranteed that he will do so.

In the Shadowscapes card, a lovely mermaid has lost interest in her fascinating surroundings. She is riveted only by her own reflection, or so it seems. While gazing into the water, rippling the surface, she may very well see something that inspires her into action. However, it is just as easy to imagine her falling into self-absorbed lethargy.

Five of Cups

It is probably impossible to go through life without loss of some sort. The Five of Cups is not about what or who has left our lives but about our experience of and reaction to that now-empty space. It represents a period of mourning. Everyone responds differently, although it is said that however grief is expressed, we all go through similar stages. The card does not say whether the grief is warranted or not, just that it is being experienced.

Five of Cups

The Universal Waite card shows the stages of grief in one image. The scene in the foreground has denial (his back is turned), anger (the cups have been kicked or knocked over), and bargaining and depression (he is hunched over with his head down). The background contains the final step of acceptance … crossing the bridge into the city to begin anew. The figure is in the middle but nearing the end of the grieving process.

Core meaning:
Experience of loss and grief.

The woman in the Legacy card is much more emotionally evocative than the Universal Waite image. Although her pain is raw and apparent, her healing is also in the image. The broken glasses show her shattered emotions and disrupted life. However, she clutches two unbroken cups, representing hope and healing. She is also in the midst of the grieving process.

In the Shadowscapes card, a woman is gazing into a bowl with a fish. With the two empty bowls at her feet and the shiny new bowl being brought to her by the water spirits, she is in the midst of her experience of loss. The circle surrounding her and including the faeries highlights the healing aspect of the grieving process.

Six of Cups

There is a saying about the past being gone, the future not yet created, so all we have is the present. However, that is not exactly true. All of our past experiences create who we are today. Our thoughts about the future direct where we will ultimately go. Although we do have happy memories, sad memories, and every sort in between, the Six of Cups is about the pleasant ones. The role those memories play in our current lives depends on the circumstances. The memory in question can be from the distant past or it could be one in the making. Like all the cards, it must be read in context.

Six of Cups

The Universal Waite card is a scene of sweet and gentle kindness. The white flowers in the cups symbolize innocent pleasures and gifts without strings. The image may strike some as being too idyllic or overly sentimental, leading some to read this card as romanticizing the past.

Core meaning:

Happy memories.

The Legacy card shows the cups in a circle, indicating that memories are a part of the circle of life. They are the continuum that ties who you were and what you experienced with your present. There is a focus here on how and where you will fit the memory in question into your circle.

The Shadowscapes card presents a scene of make-believe. This card is about adapting a childlike state, where the world is wider and more things are possible. It is not just a happy memory but also a tie to a time when our imaginations were powerful.

Seven of Cups

The great thing about imagination is that it allows us to picture so many possible options. We can build these fantastic dreams and live in them in our minds before determining which of them we want to follow. The Seven of Cups shows all of our dreams and desires laid out, awaiting our consideration. This card doesn't tell us how to choose. It expresses the feelings we have in the face of possibilities and implies the downside of this experience: until a choice is made, there is a lack of focus.

Seven of Cups

In the Universal Waite card, the figure is darkened and his back is to us, indicating confusion and distraction. The dreams are looming so large that they are casting him in a shadow. The contrast between the man and the cups is unsettling.

Core meaning:

Dreams and desires.

The Legacy image focuses on the immensity of the choices. They fill the card, lit by the sun, taking on lives of their own. The viewer isn't even in the picture. The focus is on the dazzling effect of the dreams.

The Shadowscapes card takes a different approach. In this card, a choice has been made; there is one dream and two responses to it. The woman sees it clearly and feels excited by it. The man is intent on figuring out how to achieve the dream. This shows a dream as a compass that directs decisions and actions.

Eight of Cups

We leave situations all the time and for different reasons. The Eight of Cups is about leaving the known and comfortable for the unknown. The reasons and results are different for each journey and each seeker. What is common to the experience is the promise of transformation. The act of leaving is the first step on a journey that will change us. Even if we return, we will be different, and therefore nothing will ever be the same again.

In the Universal Waite card, a man leaves his ordered rows of cups. There is clearly something missing, indicated by the open space in the top row. He seeks that missing piece. The mountains in the background imply a challenging journey, and the moon represents change and the unknown.

Core meaning:
Leaving something behind to search for something else.

The Legacy card shows the transformative aspect more clearly. The figure leaves the known, the water, in which he exists as a sea creature, and turns toward the unknown, the sky, and becomes a man. The symbolism of leaving the waters of the subconscious for the air of the rational mind affects the meaning. It indicates coming out of a fog into clarity.

The Shadowscapes card shows the same situation as the Legacy card, except in reverse. In this card, the figure is leaving the surface of the water to delve into the depths of the ocean. The journey of transformation in this card is an inward one, a searching for what lies below the surface.

Nine of Cups

In the days when playing cards were used for divination, the Nine of Hearts was called "the wish card." It meant that your wish would come true. The Nine of Cups has that same promise, although there is a fine line between having what you want and wanting what you have. Both sides of that coin are in this card. It represents feeling satisfied and happy with what you have.

Cups

9

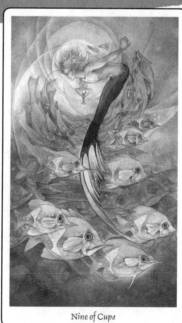

Nine of Cups

The Universal Waite card shows a very contented man sitting proudly before his fine collection of chalices. Some interpret him as smug and focused too much on his possessions. But we must consider the symbolism. The cups are on a blue-draped table, representing a spiritual and healthy aspect. The man is facing us in a sociable manner, as if welcoming us, rather than obsessing about his possessions.

Core meaning:
Material, emotional, and physical well-being.

In the Legacy card, the lush sweetness of the fruits is so real we can almost taste them. There is an abundance and variety of good things. They are at the peak of ripeness and ready to be enjoyed. The implication is that it almost would be a sin not to partake and savor these gifts.

In the Shadowscapes card, the abundance of fish represent health, prosperity, and good fortune. The focus in this card is the figure's relishing and enjoyment of his happy situation.

Ten of Cups

There are two cards that represent positive home or family lives: the Ten of Pentacles and the Ten of Cups. The former focuses on material stability. This one is about emotional stability and healthy relationships. The Ten of Cups shows the range of emotions found in a happy home: contentment, comfort, joy, playfulness, and affection. While these are generally considered positive, we should bear in mind that, for some, this scene is the very picture of boredom. Not everyone wants the same things.

Ten of Cups

In the Universal Waite card, the adults look skyward with arms upraised, acknowledging the role of the Divine, or spirituality, in their happiness. The children dance and play. The river in the card shows how their relationships flow through and nourish their lives.

Core meaning:

Happy home.

The Legacy card uses pets to illustrate the idea of unconditional love. This image focuses on warmth, comfort, and safety. The goblets represent the emotions and relationships upon which this experience is built. They shine and sparkle in the firelight, giving remarkable beauty to an everyday scene.

The Shadowscapes card focuses less on domestic bliss and more on a single, deeply emotional connection. The circle that encompasses the couple suggests safety and the joy of being in the world that they have created.

Ace of Swords

The Ace of Swords is a gift, an unexpected opportunity, a moment of fortuitous possibility. The aces show up when the time is right for action, but we must act quickly, as these moments do not last long and will soon pass us by. Whatever is initiated at this time has the potential for success.

This ace contains the airy energy of all the swords. Its energy is manifested in several ways—intellect, truth, communication, logic, decisiveness—and is excellent for problem solving, decision making, and any logical or philosophical endeavors. The Ace of Swords is a tool that helps us cut through confusion and see our way more clearly.

The Ace of Swords is a very powerful gift and can be the most dangerous. Truth can hurt, words can sting, and new ways of thinking can turn worlds upside down. The card itself doesn't speak of the outcome, only of the inherent power.

ACE of SWORDS.

Swords

Ace

Ace of Swords

The Universal Waite sword is pointing skyward, indicating a connection with the Divine and with ultimate truth. A laurel wreath and an olive branch are draped on the crown, symbolizing the two sides of the sword: victory and peace. The crown conveys the sense that mastery, skill, and responsibility are required to wield this sword.

Core meaning:
An opportunity for a new way of thinking.

The Legacy card shows a more intricate sword pointing down, indicating that the truth may not always be as simple, as clear, and as universal as we'd like, especially when applied to specific situations. The amethyst stone in the hilt represents peace of mind and mental healing. The focus here is less active: by understanding, we gain clarity and peace.

The Shadowscapes card focuses on the transformative power of a new idea or way of thinking, symbolized by the swans and the butterflies. This card speaks more of the results or ramifications than of the event itself.

Two of Swords

The heart and the mind are not always in agreement. Usually, though, one or the other is more persuasive, and so a decision is easily made. However, there are times when they are equally compelling and we find ourselves paralyzed. The Two of Swords represents this uncomfortable state. Our logical self is urging a certain choice; our intuitive self prefers a different direction. Until we decide, there is nothing to do but maintain the current situation. Unfortunately, this card does not say how long the state will last or which side will win. Because this is a sword and not a cup, the mind does have the home field advantage.

Two of Swords

The Universal Waite card shows a woman sitting on a bench holding two swords, which represent the decision she must make. The blindfold shows her reliance on logic and intellect. Behind her, the sea and moon represent the pull of her emotional side, her heart.

Core meaning:
A conflict between
heart and mind.

The Legacy card shows the balance between mind and heart through the two swords and the purple scarf flowing over her eyes. Because the pose is different from the Universal Waite image, there is less tension and more peace.

In the Shadowscapes card, the figure holds the two swords and seems ready to reject the reasons of the heart, as he refuses to look at the hanging heart or accept the flower from the swan. This card implies that the decision is difficult. The swords seem to suit the man, but the heart and flower glow with warmth and light that are strongly compelling.

Three of Swords

As mentioned in the Ace of Swords, the truth can be a wonderful, liberating experience—but it can also deeply wound. The Three of Swords is that very situation, in three stages. Something has been learned, said, or revealed that has cut us to our very core. The immediate pain is felt. Then there is recognition that the wound is fatal, at least to a certain aspect of our existence. Something has been stabbed, and it is not likely to heal. Betrayal is often associated with this card, not because it is illustrated or represented in the card, but because it is the people we know and trust who can hurt us the most.

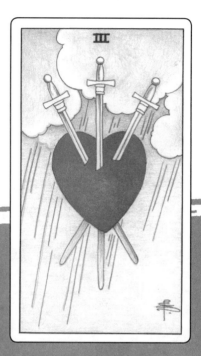

Three of Swords

This Universal Waite card is one of the easiest to interpret in the entire deck. The image is almost simplistic in its clarity. The heart of something has been stabbed, and the very heavens weep for it.

Core meaning:

Sorrow caused by knowledge.

The Legacy card poignantly and powerfully depicts the recognition of the depth and significance of the wound. The look in her eye says that she will never be the same again.

The Shadowscapes card shows a murdered swan, the death of great beauty and power. This card, more overtly than the others, speaks to betrayal. The designer of this deck points out that a swan is strong and would fight back rather than be hurt. There is no sign of struggle; therefore, we assume that someone known to the swan did this.

Four of Swords

Some troubles come in the form of a crisis that requires immediate action. Others are complex and demand much thought and reflection. In addition, they can be mentally or emotionally exhausting. In these instances, we need a time-out. This is the situation in the Four of Swords. It is a withdrawal from events to regroup. The implication in this card is that by taking this time away and quieting the mind, we may then hear a solution to our troubles.

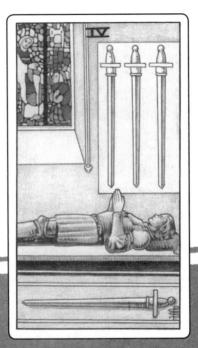

Four of Swords

The Universal Waite card shows a man lying in a church, representing a place of safety and higher wisdom. The pose and the casket remind us of death. In a sense, it is a death—the end of a problem put to rest by a practical solution.

Core meaning:

Respite from troubles.

The Legacy card also takes place in a churchlike setting. The bird is the soul receiving redemption and rebirth, symbolized by the red and white roses.

In the Shadowscapes card, the figure holds a sword to her heart and has one under her head, searching for wisdom that will quiet her soul and cut through her confusion. The lotus blossoms represent enlightenment.

Five of Swords

A Pyrrhic victory is one that comes at too great a cost. The Five of Swords is a card of victory and of loss. The victorious figure seems oblivious to the destruction and is just happy to have won. It is not clear when or if he will ever realize the price he paid, although at some point an accounting must be made. The cost of this situation is so high, some interpretations leave off the idea of victory altogether and call the card simply "defeat."

Swords

5

Five of Swords

The Universal Waite card shows no bloodshed, indicating a purely mental situation, such as manipulation or some other kind of treachery. It is as though he simply talked the others into laying down their swords. He is clearly happy with the result, but there is an implication that he has sown seeds in the others that he will reap unpleasantly later.

Core meaning:
A victory tinged with defeat.

In the Legacy card, we see a site of utter destruction. Amid raging fires and dead bodies, the victor stands holding his gain … five swords. His tattered flag remains, waving over a field of death.

The Shadowscapes card shows the premeditation before the battle. Although certainly intent on physical destruction, this card focuses on the mental aspect of planning and preparing for such an event. The black swans symbolize the dark and dangerous forces that are engaged.

Six of Swords

The Six of Swords has a melancholy feel because of the implication that there is a situation bad enough to warrant escaping. The decision to leave can feel like giving up or giving in, and it is hard to feel good about that. However, if the situation is distasteful enough, moving on is better than enduring the unendurable. We don't usually make such weighty decisions on our own. Advice and aid are often sought, and they are pictured in this card. This is not a trip we make alone.

Six of Swords

The Universal Waite card is bleak, with its icy, pale sky and hunched, cloaked passenger. But the foreground is filled with the boat and oarsman. There may be sadness, but the focus is on the escape and the help. The idea that this is a positive move is highlighted by the waves, indicating rough waters, on the right side of the boat and the smooth waters on the left. Some people believe that the presence of the swords in the boat indicates that the passengers bring their troubles with them wherever they go, but that is best determined by the context.

Core meaning:

Leaving a situation with help.

The Legacy card shows a woman facing her journey with confidence and complete faith in her helper, who is steering the boat. The swords rising from the water and coming down from the sky represent the dangers faced during this time and the difficulty of the decision.

In the Shadowscapes card, the woman riding the swan symbolizes relying on others for help. Her faith and confidence are evident by her relaxed pose. The swan takes her above and away from her troubles, indicated by the ravens perched on the swords.

Seven of Swords

This is a card about theft. Who the thief is and what has been taken may be divined by the other cards, as it is not evident here. The card hints at the possibility of his capture, but more so at the idea of karmic retribution rather than social justice. The item being taken may be tangible, but because this is a swords card, it may be intangible, such as an idea, confidence, or freedom.

Seven of Swords

In the Universal Waite card, the thief is brightly dressed and prancing around in the daylight. He is not making any attempt at stealth. In addition, he leaves behind two swords, which can easily be used against him by any pursuers. The focus seems to be on the stupidity of the thief.

Core meaning:
Someone has taken something.

The Legacy card shows a stealthy thief working under the cover of night. No matter how clever he is, he probably doesn't realize there is a witness—the magpie. Because this is a bird and not a human, it hints at a more natural law and karmic retribution.

The Shadowscapes card shows a thief admiring his bounty. Feeling hidden in the darkness and behind a rock, he, like the Legacy thief, is unaware of a witness to his actions. He believes he has gotten away with something, but the swan seems to think otherwise.

Eight of Swords

The Eight of Swords is the feeling of being in a position that is dangerous on several levels. First, it feels as if any move we make leads to a problem or roadblock of some sort, or even makes the situation worse. There appear to be no viable options. Second, we feel inhibited and blind. We cannot move with our normal nimbleness, nor can we see the whole situation. A bad situation is made worse by the feeling of helplessness.

Eight of Swords

The Universal Waite image is so static that it almost feels serene. Is she calmly reviewing possible plans to escape, or is she resigned to her fate? She seems to be in no immediate danger, although she is unable to make any progress. The focus of this card is not as much on danger as it is on feeling immobilized.

Core meaning:

A precarious situation.

The Legacy card shows more movement. The woman seems to be struggling in a web. Her every movement brings the swords closer. Although her arms are not bound, she is blindfolded. Also, she is nearly naked, indicating vulnerability. This card shows a more immediately dangerous and difficult situation.

The Shadowscapes card echoes the danger and helplessness depicted in the Legacy card. The more the swan flails about, the more entangled he becomes. The small hummingbird provides a hint of hope and perhaps even rescue.

Nine of Swords

Although we may try not to worry needlessly or do things we will regret, having concerns and making mistakes we wish we hadn't are natural parts of life. The Nine of Swords is about what happens when worries or regrets become obsessive—when we don't let them go, when we feed them with our thoughts. In this card, the original concern is no longer the issue; rather, the issue is the effect the obsessing is having on *us*. It overwhelms us and permeates our view. It colors everything, getting in the way of our progress and potentially controlling our futures. The implication is that these effects are negative or at best neutral and hold no positive results.

Nine of Swords

The Universal Waite card shows a person who should be resting her mind and body by sleeping. Instead, problems or concerns keep her up, robbing her of the refreshment and healing time of slumber.

Core meaning:
The power of worry and regret.

The Legacy card is more ominous. The swords represent her worries taking on a life of their own, becoming hands that are reaching toward her mind. They will shape her thoughts, which will eventually affect her feelings and actions.

In the Shadowscapes card, the figure has already internalized the thought patterns created by the obsessive worries or concerns, as symbolized by the tattoos on his chest. The crows come down from the sky, representing the downward spiral that results in this case.

Ten of Swords

When things are not going our way, we usually try to change them. In many cases, we can. But we do not have total control over the world and cannot deny that sometimes things we consider bad, unpleasant, or unfortunate do happen. The Ten of Swords clearly shows that something has gone badly wrong. But more specifically, it shows the point of giving in, giving up, or surrendering. We may have tried valiantly to fix the situation or called it quits at the first sign of trouble. The main point is that the decision has been made to cease.

Ten of Swords

The Universal Waite card shows someone who is completely done in. The lack of actual blood in the picture reminds us that this is symbolic and not literal. He has not died; he's just taken all he's going to take. And so, he lies down and waits for the sunrise. There is more a sense of relief and calmness than of tragedy or sadness.

Core meaning:
Surrender to unpleasant or unfortunate circumstances.

In the Legacy card, the scene is much different. This man is railing and struggling. He is not going quietly at all. The situation may be over, but he's not done torturing himself about it.

The Shadowscapes card is one of grace and elegance. The woman has quit struggling and let go. Although apparently falling from a great height, she seems unworried, trusting that all will turn out okay in the end.

Ace of Pentacles

Like all of the aces, the Ace of Pentacles is a gift or unexpected opportunity. The aces indicate a moment in time filled with fortuitous possibility. The power of the aces shows up in our lives when circumstances are just right for action. Acting quickly is the best way to take advantage of the aces, as these moments do not last long. If we don't take advantage of the opportunity, it passes us by. Aces are also seeds of great promise. Whatever is planted or initiated at this time has the potential for success.

Because this is a pentacles card, it contains the earthy energy of all the pentacles. This energy is manifested in several ways: material items, resources, health, security, abundance. It is particularly suited for financial activities, anything tangible, and sensual pleasures. The Ace of Pentacles is the universe's way of saying "This is your lucky day!"

Arthur Edward Waite wrote that this card is "the most favorable of all cards."

ACE of PENTACLES

Coins

Ace

Ace of Pentacles

The Universal Waite card shows the hand of the universe presenting a pentacle. It is a seed with perhaps more potential than the other aces, as it carries within it the promise of manifestation. The idea that this seed can grow abundantly is symbolized by the garden.

Core meaning:

An opportunity for prosperity.

The Legacy card is filled with the promise of prosperity. The acorn represents potential. The bees symbolize growth and fruitfulness, and the hedgehog, protection and resourcefulness. Everything that is needed is available in this moment.

The Shadowscapes card presents the gift of the pentacle in a lush setting, in an area ready to support growth. The lizards promise good fortune. The arrangement of the trees and wood spirits indicate protection and security.

Two of Pentacles

When this card comes up, it is easy to think of multi-tasking. Doing several things at once is common for most of us, at least sometimes. There are hectic times when everything we are attempting threatens to fall. But then there are those times when everything goes amazingly smoothly, almost like magic. The Two of Pentacles is that kind of balancing. We are directing rather than controlling. We are in a Zen-like state. We are working with the flow of the universe. The card is not necessarily about doing things but about balancing the flow of our lives in a graceful and natural way.

Coins

2

Two of Pentacles

The Universal Waite card shows the idea of being in sync with the universe in two ways. The ships flow up and down on the waves, working with the sea while making forward progress. The pentacles being juggled are within a lemniscate, which symbolizes the eternal flow of the universe.

Core meaning:
Maintaining balance.

The Legacy card has a whimsical quality, with its colorfully dressed figure showing that such a state is enjoyable. Riding a penny-farthing bicycle over water indicates that operating in a playful way allows accomplishments that may seem impossible.

In the Shadowscapes card, the figure is reminiscent of the god Shiva, Lord of Destruction, but known precisely as the Lord of Change. This card takes a broader look at the idea of universal balance—in particular, the delicate balance between destruction and creation.

Three of Pentacles

It has been said that the four suits of the tarot represent what is needed to make something happen. Wands represent the inspiration; cups, the desire; swords, the plan; and pentacles, the actual physical manifestation. The Three of Pentacles often includes all those aspects but always focuses on the actual physical item being created. This card represents the partial completion of a work in progress. There is something to be shown for the energy already invested. There is still time to make tweaks and changes. Things are coming into focus.

Three of Pentacles

The Universal Waite card shows three figures. Two are holding plans and represent the swords mentioned above. The artisan is discussing the project with the others and getting feedback or direction. The inclusion of three figures and the discussion of the work in progress highlight the idea of teamwork, or working together to achieve something. Notice, though, that the artisan is elevated above the two others, a reminder that in this card, he is the main character.

Core meaning:

A goal is manifesting.

The Legacy card features a close-up of an artist working intently on his project. His attention is on the process, on what he's doing. There are no other figures or even any evidence of plans or directions. The focus is clearly on the act of creating and of revealing, bit by bit, what is being created.

In the Shadowscapes card, a woman and man work as one. The man holds the salamander, or the seed of the idea, and supports the woman. She focuses the energy that creates the art. Here, as in the Universal Waite card, there is teamwork. And like the Universal Waite, there is also an elevation of the artist, meaning that the focus is on the creator and creation.

Four of Pentacles

The idea of gathering power often has negative connotations. We associate it with ideas of being "power hungry," seeking power to control others, or gaining power through the exploitation of others. But to read this card in that way reflects possibly erroneous assumptions and personal judgments. This card is about gathering power, for whatever reason and through whatever means. Unlike the Two of Pentacles, where energy flowed, in the Four of Pentacles, the energy is not flowing. It is being held in reserve for future use. This power can be realized through many ways, such as money, control over resources, a secure or safe living environment, or acquiring the ability to earn a living. Whether the means and the end yield a happy situation remains to be seen.

Four of Pentacles

In the Universal Waite card, the man's entire focus is on gathering or holding on to his power. It is on his mind, as shown by the pentacle on his head. It is in his heart, as shown by the pentacle in his arms. It is his foundation, as shown by the pentacles under his feet. His being outside the town with his power represents that these resources are at present outside of the flow of goods.

Core meaning:

Gathering power.

The Legacy card is a close-up of the man and his coins, representing his power. He has it all in hand and held close, giving a feeling of hoarding or selfishness, although really we don't know what his plans are. His expression is enigmatic and can be read as cautiously pleased, frightened, or obsessively protective.

The Shadowscapes card takes the idea of hoarding and selfishness and runs with it. The dragon is a symbol for greed and obsessive love of treasure. He also represents the sort of paranoia that thinks everyone is out to take what is his. This card, unlike the others, overtly highlights the negative side of power.

Five of Pentacles

Physical needs represented by the Five of Pentacles come in many varieties. The need can be financial, health related, or, perhaps, looking for help moving furniture. Or they could be more basic: somewhere to sleep, something to eat, something to wear. The Five of Pentacles card usually includes an indication that help is close at hand, so the situation, while unpleasant, is likely not dire. The card also often suggests that the person in need is not noticing the help or opportunities available.

Five of Pentacles

In the Universal Waite card, the figures are clearly in need, as shown by the crutches, ragged clothing, and lack of shoes on a snowy night. They are walking past a church, symbolizing a resource for help, yet they walk past as if not noticing it. It is unknown whether they are consciously ignoring that option for some reason or they just don't see it.

Core meaning:
Physical need.

The Legacy card shows a woman begging. Her expression is desolate, but also stubborn and demanding. The church window shines in the background. As in the Universal Waite card, we are left to wonder why she does not turn in that direction.

The Shadowscapes card shows a distraught woman outside a colorful church window and surrounded by beautiful abundance. Being so wrapped up in her need, she sees none of it.

Six of Pentacles

In the Two of Pentacles, we saw the flow of material energy as directed by ourselves within our own lives. In the Four of Pentacles, we saw the stopping of that flow. In the Six of Pentacles, we see a different kind of flow—from one person (or organization) to another. This happens through gifts, donations, scholarships, etc. This card is about giving and receiving. The balance between the two acts is so delicate that it is sometimes hard to tell which is which, and the cards often reflect this. This card doesn't say who is doing the giving or receiving; it indicates simply that material energy is being exchanged.

Six of Pentacles

The Universal Waite card shows an apparently wealthy man holding a set of scales as he doles out his charity. This image has often rubbed modern tarot readers the wrong way. They don't like the idea that he gets to judge anyone's needs and assume that he is judging the other people's worth. Actually, the set of scales symbolizes the balance between giving and receiving—that it is not a one-sided relationship.

Core meaning:
Flowing material energy.

The Legacy card includes a set of scales as well, and one hand giving to two hands. Showing the hands without faces takes the individual out of the picture and in some ways makes the idea less humiliating and more palatable. The focus in this image is on the flow of material energy, pure and simple, and not on any potential human emotions, reactions, or motivations.

The Shadowscapes card presents a more abstract image. The musician plays and thus causes coins to flow. The coins nourish the plant below. And in its turn, the plant inspires the musician. The focus in this card is the endless and connected cycle of the flow of material goods.

Seven of Pentacles

Once we've been working at something for a while, there comes a time when we take a step back and look at the results. We think about the effort invested. We consider our expectations. We see where things are at. The Seven of Pentacles represents this time of judgment and appraisal. Before continuing on with the project, we want to be sure it's moving at an acceptable rate and in an acceptable manner. If things are not meeting our expectations, there are many options (such as quitting, lowering expectations, or doing things differently), but none are actually given in the card.

Seven of Pentacles

The Universal Waite card shows a man examining the pentacles growing on a vine. He is quietly considering all that he sees. Although the harvest appears lush and bountiful, his calm expression shows neither satisfaction nor disappointment.

Core meaning:
Appraising results of efforts.

The Legacy card shows a woman examining her harvest, still hanging from the tree. Her expression is more obviously satisfied. She holds an empty basket at the ready, symbolizing her confidence that she will gather this fruit.

In the Shadowscapes card, the woman has already begun harvesting. She is carefully and closely searching the as-yet unready fruit. The tattoos on her arm and chest show how fully she identifies herself with this particular project.

Eight of Pentacles

The Eight of Pentacles embodies the saying that practice makes perfect. This card represents diligent repetition until it is done right and suggests that "good enough" isn't actually good enough. There is a commitment to making it the best, including making sure every detail is correct. Although there is a sense of beauty and art, there is more attention to the technical aspects of the work. Another saying comes to mind with this card: any job worth doing is worth doing well.

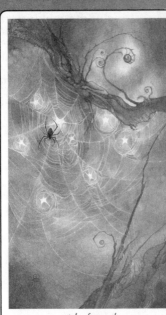

Eight of Pentacles

The Universal Waite card shows a craftsman turning out the same pentacle over and over again. Any changes or improvements are not apparent. The idea here is that repetition has made perfect, and now each one he creates is the best.

In the Legacy card, the craftsman is not quite happy yet with his results. He is reviewing notes and using instruments to make sure everything goes together as it should. He is not doing the same design over and over again until he gets it right; he is trying new designs over and over again until he discovers the perfect design.

The Shadowscapes card expresses the idea of beautiful, practical design with a spider web. While the web is artistic, there is less focus on technical perfection in this card.

Nine of Pentacles

Enjoying beauty and abundance is generally considered a good thing. When that experience is the result of our own work, there is an even deeper pleasure. It is often difficult to tell which is more gratifying—the thing itself or our pride in having achieved it. The experience is our own private celebration, for we've done well and we know it. We are our own judge, and there is no need for external validation. The Nine of Pentacles represents a situation filled with personal satisfaction as well as the sensual enjoyment of the results of diligence and discipline.

Nine of Pentacles

The Universal Waite card features the richness of the accomplishment with a well-dressed woman in a lush garden. The falcon and grapevines symbolize discipline and hard work.

Core meaning:

Accomplishment.

The Legacy card shows a bird of paradise, representing closeness to the Divine, instead of a falcon, eliminating the idea of disciplined achievement. Instead, it evokes the idea of blending the spiritual, or higher, impulses with the physical.

The Shadowscapes card retains the idea of discipline with a piano player. Through study and practice, she creates wondrous music, uniting the physical with the spiritual.

Ten of Pentacles

The Ten of Pentacles is what the Ace of Pentacles wants to be when it grows up. In this card, all the promise and possibility of the ace is manifested. Financial abundance and domestic security are there, of course. In addition, though, there is something more, a deeper gift. In some way, this abundance is connected to our roots, our past, or our ancestors as well as to our future and our legacy. It is said that the past is over and the future is yet to come, and therefore we should focus on the present, an idea also discussed in the Six of Cups. However, being able to look back with pride on past accomplishments and look ahead with confidence make the present even more wonderful.

Ten of Pentacles

The Universal Waite card has a young couple in the center, representing the present. The child represents the future, while the older man is the past. The dogs are faithfulness and loyalty. The pentacles, banners, and arch symbolize material achievement and prosperity.

Core meaning:

Stable and abundant life.

The Legacy card shows the idea of a legacy, family money, or inheritance with the chest of coins and jewels. The tulips also symbolize wealth and prosperity. Unlike the coins and jewels, tulips are fragile and need tending and nurturing, much like a family and home.

In the Shadowscapes card, a young woman leans against a dragon, which symbolizes her inner strength and power. She holds a peach, representing the gifts she has been given. Partnering with her dragonself and using her gifts wisely, she has created her dream, the castle in the distance.

The Court Cards

These cards represent the actions of people that influence our lives. And like actual people, the court cards can feel hard to understand. Focusing on the role that someone plays or the action they take regarding a situation rather than on their personality makes interpreting these cards in a reading much easier and more useful. We understand what is going on and also gain practical information about how to work with those involved in the situation.

The roles played are determined by rank: page, knight, queen, or king. The rank also determines the extent of influence the person has on the situation. For example, the ramifications of the actions of a page will be very different from that of a king. Rank also indicates how easily you can enlist the support of or change the actions of a person represented by that court card. Again, you are likely to have an easier time talking a page into doing something than a king. By paying attention to the card's suit, you get a hint about their motivations and priorities, helping you understand the best way to approach that particular person.

By necessity, the images in the court cards are either male or female. There are traditions regarding which gender to use on which card, but modern designers play with these traditions. In the following text, I'll use the traditional pronoun for the general discussion and the pronoun that matches the card for the individual card discussions. The cards, however, can represent a person of either gender.

The Pages

When a page appears in a reading, it indicates someone who needs help or guidance. A page can also provide support that will affect the development of the situation.

The young, fresh-faced pages are feeling the first flush of excitement and trepidation that accompanies all new experiences. They may not literally be young people, but rather they are people who feel young because they are in a new situation. They are just getting the hang of something, figuring out how something works or feels to them, or determining whether the thing in question is right for them. To others, they may appear skeptical or resistant, as they spend time assessing the situation before fully committing. In short, they are observing and learning before deciding.

Pages generally do not have powerful or far-reaching influence. It is unlikely that they, by a decision or action, can upset or radically alter the querent's life. Instead, they are more likely to request the querent's help or support. They can bring enthusiasm and freshness to a situation. And although they are not commonly considered powerful, they can be a great support and help. Not only that, but they are generally eager to be engaged in projects. They are willing to help in order to be part of something larger.

All the pages share curiosity, skepticism, courage, and fear. They all may feel slightly off-balance and grateful for support or guidance. In exchange, they can offer loyalty and enthusiasm. Each page is also very different, as we shall soon see.

Page of Wands

The Page of Wands is someone who has just discovered (or rediscovered) his sense of self, has experienced (or re-experienced) something inspiring or has just learned about (or relearned) what fuels his passion. Whatever this thing is, it is represented by the wand. At this point, he knows what it is and has some idea of its power but has not yet grasped all the ramifications. He is still getting used to the idea, playing out scenarios in his mind and imagining possibilities. This experience bestows a sense of power and self-determination. He may find this either freeing or frightening, but more likely both.

PAGE of WANDS.

Page of Wands

Page of Wands

The Universal Waite page holds his wand at a distance, not quite embracing it. He admires and examines it. He sees it as something separate from himself. Before exploring how to use it, he wishes to understand it objectively.

Core meaning:
One who is assessing something in the areas of will, inspiration, or passion.

The page in the Legacy card holds his wand close, with a defiant expression. He is already asserting ownership. He seems to know he definitely wants to own all that the wand promises and symbolizes. However, he also looks as though he hopes he won't be called upon to use his newly acquired wands energy just yet.

The Shadowscapes page is bolder than the other two. She immediately takes up her wand (the bow of the violin) and tries it out. She wants to see what it is capable of in her hands. This experience fills her, and she loses herself in it.

Page of Cups

The Page of Cups represents someone who is seeing as if for the first time a matter of the heart, such as a relationship, emotion, or creative impetus, which is represented by the cup. He may have any number of reactions: enchanted, beguiled, curious, hesitant, repulsed, confused. But this card is not necessarily concerned with his immediate reaction. What it does reveal is that he does not know what to do with the experience. He has acknowledged its existence but is not sure what he is prepared to do with it or how it relates to him and his life. Instead of taking action, he prefers to examine and study it, seeking its secrets and searching for understanding before making any decisions.

PAGE of CUPS.

Page of Cups

Page of Cups

In the Universal Waite card, the page has already made some progress in understanding the situation. The fish peeking out of the cup is revealing a secret. The page appears pleased with what he is learning. He holds the cup away from him, making clear that he is keeping it at arm's length for now, at least. His approach is one of objective study.

Core meaning:
One who is assessing something
in the area of emotions,
relationships, or art.

The Legacy page gently holds the glass goblet close and caresses it. He does not look at it but examines it through tentative experience. He is looking forward, as if asking for guidance, direction, or someone to share the experience. This approach is more hands-on, literally and figuratively.

The Shadowscapes card has more emphasis on the page losing herself in the experience. She lets it fill her. She wants to know how it feels. However, she is doing this alone, in a place where she feels comfortable and safe.

Page of Swords

The Page of Swords is someone who is encountering a new idea, solution, way of thinking, or method of communication, which is represented by the sword. At the moment, although he acknowledges the idea, he neither discounts nor fully accepts it. He needs to spend some time with this new concept. First, he needs to determine whether or not he thinks it is theoretically true. Then he wants to know how this metaphorical sword can be applied to his life in practical terms. And finally, he will decide how useful it will be.

PAGE of SWORDS.

Page of Swords

Page of Swords

In the Universal Waite card, the page has taken up the sword to get a feel for it. He takes a swing, strikes a pose; he wants to know how it fits with him. Is it something that he can use effectively? Does it seem true and balanced in his hand?

Core meaning:
One who is assessing something
in the area of ideas, systems,
or communication.

The Legacy page presents the swords as if looking for input or opinions. The two swords, as opposed to the more traditional single sword, show that she recognizes the double-edged aspect. Instead of touching them directly, she carries them carefully on a pillow, acknowledging their potential danger.

The Shadowscapes card shows the page settling in for a long test drive. The swan represents the momentum and long-term ramifications of using the sword. The page lets herself be lifted and carried. However, her focus is on the rabbit in her lap. While she wants to see where this will take her, she also wants to see how it affects the smaller things in her life.

Page of Pentacles

The Page of Pentacles is someone who has received something new, such as a material item, a resource, or money (or a way to earn money), which is represented by the pentacle. For him, this item is worth far more than it appears. In it, he sees possibilities. He is imagining how he can make the best use of it. More than likely, he will parlay this opportunity into more than anyone else would imagine. Whether or not this actually happens is uncertain, but he is certainly going to try.

PAGE of PENTACLES

Page of Coins

Page of Pentacles

The Universal Waite card shows the page barely holding the pentacle, as if he doesn't want to squash any of the potential within or as if he regards it as a delicate, precious gift. He gazes into it, mesmerized by the universes of possibilities he sees.

Core meaning:
One who is assessing something in the area of the physical world, resources, or finances.

The page in the Legacy card holds her pentacle firmly and proudly. She knows she has a treasure, and she is simply daring anyone to doubt her and her plans.

The Shadowscapes page does not focus on the mere material aspect, symbolized by the dragon. She sees not the thing itself but its shining potential. She finds and takes the illuminated essence. This is what she will use. This is how she will achieve things that others may not. The owl's presence indicates that this is a wise approach.

The Knights

When a knight appears in a reading, it means that someone will take swift and decisive action that will affect the situation.

Committed to following whatever holy grail they are serving at the moment, the knights rush about, incredibly focused and almost blind to everything else going on around them.

They are in the middle of pursuing a goal that may or may not have anything to do with the querent. However, during their pursuit of that goal, the knights may wreak havoc in the situation. They can be unpredictable, extreme, and chaotic. Keep an eye on them!

The best way to keep a knight from running roughshod over everything is to get their attention focused on something productive. In the right circumstances, knights can have a powerful effect on a situation, if only in the amount of energy they bring. However, it is not easy to wrangle a knight. But if you understand what motivates him, you stand a good chance of enlisting his support. Get him interested in your cause, and you will have a commanding champion in your corner.

The knights all share a love of action, a strong sense of commitment, and extreme amounts of energy. They can be dangerous and unpredictable, but they are great assets if part of your team. Each knight brings his own unique personality, motivations, and faults to any situation. Let's get up close and personal with these intriguing characters.

Knight of Wands

The Knight of Wands is someone whose actions in this situation are fired by his will. He has something very specific he wants to achieve; he very much wants to have his way and will stop at nothing to get it. The knight is all hepped up and passionate about something, and he may heedlessly run roughshod over anyone in his way. If his will is in sync with the querent's, he will be a helpful influence; if not, the querent could get run over. Such intensity is often not maintained for very long, so it may be possible to just ride out this burst of energy.

Knight of Wands

The Universal Waite knight is focused and directed. He is moving quickly. All that matters to him is getting there … wherever "there" is. He holds his wand, representing his will, as evidence that he is clearly right. His rearing horse symbolizes his intense energy—an energy he can barely control.

Core meaning:
One who acts in the realm of will, inspiration, or passion.

In the Legacy card, the knight is identifying himself entirely with the current situation. The dragons represent his will and passion, both of which are fired up and determined to win.

In the Shadowscapes card, the lion symbolizes the idea that the knight thinks he is king of the jungle. He believes he is right and strong and brave and that he must prevail.

Knight of Cups

The Knight of Cups is someone whose current actions in this situation are motivated by emotion. His heart is focused on something, such as a vision, a quest, a creation, or on someone. In this case, he is absolutely compelled to follow his heart to the exclusion of all else, for good or ill. At this point, he considers nothing else; all that matters is his presumed love, reconciliation, poetry, art, or dream. It will be very difficult to turn this knight's attention from his current pursuit.

KNIGHT of CUPS.

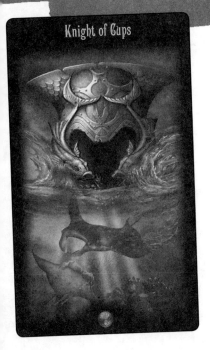

Knight of Cups

Knight of Cups

The Universal Waite knight is so certain of his heart's message that he moves slowly and steadily forward toward his dream. He has a firm grasp of his vision, as symbolized by his holding the cup. This clarity allows him to progress. It is his compass.

Core meaning:
One who acts in the realm of emotions, art, and relationships.

The Legacy card shows the helmet emerging from the water, representing the knight's journey into the depths of his heart. He finds strength and direction after having been immersed in his dream.

In the Shadowscapes card, the knight's dream has taken on mystical proportions, as shown by the grail-like chalice in the sky. He is willing to follow it anywhere, whether or not it is practical or even possible.

Knight of Swords

The Knight of Swords is someone whose actions in this situation are motivated by the commitment to an idea or a way of thinking. This person believes very strongly that his idea, decision, or belief system is the right one. He will use his skill with language and communication to do all he can to further his ideal. His weapons are logic, rational arguments, and evidence. He is prepared to use them to destroy any opposition. Because he moves so quickly, he will likely flail about dangerously, lacking in a larger plan or strategy. However, if you can catch his attention and get him focused on something, he will prove invaluable.

KNIGHT of SWORDS .

Knight of Swords

Knight of Swords

The **Universal Waite knight** is a blur of fast and furious movement, as shown by his horse. He wants to move toward his goal, heedless of anyone or anything in his way. His speed and momentum are part of his power. His wildly brandished sword shows that in using speed, he likely forfeits the advantage of good strategy or tactics.

Core meaning:
One who acts in the realm of ideas, systems, or communication.

The **Legacy knight's** commitment to his ideal has become his whole identity. The wings on his helmet are reminiscent of a bird of prey. As such, he is ready to swoop in and destroy any weaker creature—or, in this case, arguments. This characteristic is echoed in the tornado destroying everything in its path. A tornado moves at terrifying speeds and very randomly, indicating a lack of game plan or strategy.

The **Shadowscapes knight** presents an image quite different from the Universal Waite and Legacy knights. This knight sits above the chaos and confusion, preferring to see things with more clarity. Instead of rushing in, he looks at the big picture, seeking the simplest and most effective solution.

Knight of Pentacles

The Knight of Pentacles is someone whose actions are motivated by resources, finances, or the material world. Whatever he does is in order to further that goal. In this area, timing can be everything, so he watches for just the right moment. He knows it's not just what you have and how you use it, but *when* you use it. He has the stamina and patience for the long haul. Although sometimes appearing passive or even weak, he is anything but. Alert and smart, he knows the value of active observation. When the time is right, he will make his move, and he rarely takes a misstep. Of all the knights, he is the most reliable for a long-term project.

KNIGHT of PENTACLES.

Knight of Coins

Knight of Pentacles

The Universal Waite knight's still horse represents stability and security as well as great reserves of power and impeccable training. This knight is focused on his goal, staying still until the moment is right.

Core meaning:
One who acts in the realm
of the physical world,
resources, or finances.

The horses in the Legacy card show the natural power available to the knight; the horns indicate that it is determination and ability. The helmet nearly blends into the background. This knight can make himself almost invisible when necessary. He can observe unnoticed until he is ready to act.

The knight in the Shadowscapes card sees his goal in the distance. The lights hanging from the trees indicate the prize is near, but he holds his dragon still. He does not rush and grasp. He considers the situation carefully before moving forward.

The Queens

When a queen appears in a reading, it means that there is someone in the querent's life who can provide needed help and advice.

Finding a queen in a reading is like finding a fairy godmother. More than any of the other court cards, the queens actually want to help the querent, and they have the wisdom—and sometimes the power—to do so. They often wield a quiet, behind-the-scenes influence that is nevertheless formidable. Not only are they willing and able to assist, they can do so in different ways. They are founts of good advice based on maturity, experience, and accomplishment. They are also skilled and able to provide valuable services.

A queen's sway may not always be easy to see or quantify. A quiet word in the right "someone's" ear here, a small act at the right time there. These nearly invisible actions can yield important results. Gaining her favor is not always easy, though. Queens may inexplicably take a liking to someone, solicitously offering help. Or they could just as easily take a dislike to someone, playing the role of an enemy instead. Part of the queen's allure and mystique is that she is like an iceberg: most of her power works below the surface.

All the queens can play the role of friend, mentor, cheerleader, and role model. They enjoy being recognized for their skills and experience. In exchange, they can offer advice and help. Each queen has her own areas of specialty.

Queen of Wands

The Queen of Wands is someone with a strong sense of self who wishes to inspire or help the querent. She understands the importance of personal power and strength of will. She can either encourage the querent to boldness or force the querent into action. She is strong and confident and wants others to be, too, whether they are ready or not. The Queen of Wands is involved in this situation because doing so furthers her own agenda. If she were to give one piece of advice, it would be this: *just do it*.

QUEEN of WANDS.

Queen of Wands

Queen of Wands

The Universal Waite queen appears almost masculine, symbolizing her assertive (verging on aggressive) nature. The sunflower represents her optimism. She looks off in the distance, scanning the horizon for opportunities, but her black cat, symbolizing her intuitive side, stares at the querent. This queen is paying attention to everything.

Core meaning:
One who develops and cares for others in the realm of will, inspiration, or passion.

The Legacy queen is bold and daring. She is clearly challenging the querent to do something, and yet there is also an encouraging compassion in her eyes. She knows the situation may be scary, but it's okay … do it anyway.

In the Shadowscapes card, the queen uses her gift of music to inspire others. She expresses the idea that if you fill yourself with the music of the spheres, you will find the courage to do anything.

Queen of Cups

The Queen of Cups is someone who wishes to develop or nurture a relationship, or to relate to, care for, or support a person on an emotional level in this situation. She is personally and emotionally involved or invested, generally in a healthy way. She feels, senses, or intuits the energies in the situation. Her guidance can be invaluable to the querent and is usually emotional, psychic, or creative in nature. This queen is generally supportive and helpful and can play the role of a patroness. If she were to give one piece of advice, it would be this: *follow your heart*.

QUEEN of CUPS.

Queen of Cups

Queen of Cups

The Universal Waite queen is observing an intricate chalice, representing her interest in observing the complexities of relationships. She is above the water rather than immersed in it, showing that while her understanding goes deep, she can view the situation from a distance, providing a bigger picture and some objectivity.

Core meaning:
One who develops and cares for others in the realm of emotions, art, or relationships.

The Legacy queen shows a comfort with water, representing the flow of emotions. She makes it seems effortless, knowing just how to move within the situation to create the movement, or results, she wants. Because she is in the water, her knowledge of such things is experiential and not merely intellectual.

In the Shadowscapes card, the queen's hair forms a lemniscate, symbolizing the infinite ebb and flow of emotions. Unafraid and completely confident, she walks across the waters of emotions, trailing sparks of light to help others find their way through the sometimes murky depths.

Queen of Swords

The Queen of Swords is someone who can help or advise about an idea, problem, communication issue, or strategy. She is smart and experienced by having lived through both good times and bad. She will have ideas and advice about how to best achieve a goal. Consult her when working on a plan. She is particularly adept at exposing deceit and seeing the truth of a matter, and she will express these plainly. She likely has her own agenda and can alter reality with a few well-chosen words. Double-check her suggestions against your own logic before jumping in. If she were to give one piece of advice, it would be this: *you need a plan, so here's what we'll do…*

QUEEN of SWORDS.

Queen of Swords

Queen of Swords

The Universal Waite queen shows an exaltation of the mind and logic. She resembles the figure of Justice, indicating her ability to cut through any mess and determine clearly what must be done. The birds and butterflies symbolize her high and lofty thoughts. She sits on higher ground, among the clouds, showing that a mind put to good use is unclouded and able to see clearly.

Core meaning:
One who develops and cares for others in the realm of ideas, systems, or communication.

The Legacy queen shows the dangerous side of logic and words. She can cut through any chaos and reveal the crux of an issue. She will see the clearest, if not the kindest, solution.

In the Shadowscapes card, the queen sees all things through the lens of logic, as represented by the sword she holds before her face. The transformative power of truth is indicated by the butterflies. She is also farsighted, symbolized by the swan, which starts out as an ugly duckling but in time reveals its powerful beauty.

Queen of Pentacles

The Queen of Pentacles is someone who can get things done in an efficient manner with a beautiful or pleasing end result. In performing tasks, she is not as elaborate as the Queen of Cups, as elegant as the Queen of Swords, or as fast as the Queen of Wands, but all the details will be attended to and all resources will be used to their fullest potential. She can help the querent with any plans that require attention to detail or making the most of something. She has a knack for turning trash into treasure and making a bad situation as comfortable as possible. If she were to give one piece of advice, it would be this: *don't worry, you* can *do this*.

QUEEN of PENTACLES

Queen of Coins

Queen of Pentacles

The Universal Waite queen sits in a lush, comfortable, prosperous garden. The rabbit represents fertility. The earth and water symbolize fruitfulness. This queen is one of nourishment and abundance.

Core meaning:
One who develops and cares for others in the realm of the physical world, resources, or finances.

The Legacy queen knows the secret to efficient achievement: visualization. See what you want; have it on your mind; have it behind you, before you, and below you; and keep the image close to your heart, as shown by the pentacles in the image. See what you want clearly, and let every step you take bring you closer to it.

The Shadowscapes card shows a queen with a deep-rooted connection to the earth. She is stable, like a tree. And like a tree, she is also a conduit for energy. She takes the soil, water, and sunlight and transforms them into something of material magnificence.

The Kings

When a king appears in a reading, it means that someone with authority will affect the outcome of the situation.

These four powerful figures have a lot in common. Most importantly, they all have authority. They all make decisions; they all delegate; they all have responsibility for other individuals or for groups; their actions have ramifications and consequences for others. Kings have achieved some level of mastery, expertise, and accomplishment. They are concerned with maintaining the status quo, at least to some extent. For many people, the kings are also father figures.

Kings may very well be making decisions that will directly affect the querent's life. Jobs may be lost or gained. Opportunities may be granted. Laws may be enacted that determine whether or not a querent can live as she pleases. Loans may be approved or denied. An insurance company may approve or deny a medical treatment. Scholarships may be given or withheld. Any of these would significantly alter a querent's life. It is likely that these decisions will be made without direct conversation with the querent. Gaining access to a king isn't always easy, and once gained, it must be used in the most effective way possible.

Kings have authority. The impact of their decisions is significant. Their ability to be influenced is limited. The role they play in a situation is that of making decisions that are to some extent outside of the querent's influence and will significantly affect the querent's situation. These are the things all kings have in common. Despite sharing so many traits, they are also as different as the four suits.

King of Wands

The influence of the King of Wands is felt in business, particularly as it pertains to entrepreneurship. He can be found in roles such as advisor, consultant, or politician. The King of Wands responds to passion and ideas. Furthermore, he is motivated by achieving his own goals. If the querent hopes to influence him, seek his support on a project, or change his mind, she should point out how her plan or idea will help him achieve his own goals, incorporate his own passion, or use his own energy and/or resources in an exciting way. He does not respond as well to emotional pleas, excruciatingly reasoned arguments, or bottom lines. Spark his creative and energetic interest, though, and you will have his attention. However, his attention will be short-lived, so make the most of it.

King of Wands

The Universal Waite king looks as if he is trying very hard to stay seated, as if he'd rather jump up and do something, representing his preference for action and indicating a bent toward hasty decisions.

Core meaning:
One who has authority, makes decisions, or is a professional in the realm of will, inspiration, or passion.

The Legacy king worships at an altar with fire on it. This represents what he values and respects. The horns on the altar form a circle, indicating a broader view. He couples his will with a grander vision.

The Shadowscapes king has fully embodied his ideals and role, as shown by his tattoo and his horns. He sees himself as being in control of his inner lion.

King of Cups

The King of Cups follows his heart and is moved by the hearts of others. Therefore, he can be found serving in areas such as counseling, health care, human services, the arts, and nonprofit organizations. Make no mistake, though: while sensitive and compassionate, this person is not a pushover. As any king, he is accomplished and wields authority. He always feels his responsibility keenly. To enlist his support and influence his decisions, appeal to his sense of tolerance and the greater good. Childish, emotional outbursts will not have the desired effect. Temper pure emotion with wisdom and experience to gain his ear.

KING of CUPS.

King of Cups

King of Cups

The Universal Waite king holds his cup casually. He is used to it, and while he values it, he is not obsessed with it. He moves across the water with confidence. Both sides of this king are shown in the images on either side of his throne. The fish (on the left) represents his emotional, creative side; the boat (on the right), his business, or professional, side.

Core meaning:
One who has authority, makes decisions, or is a professional in the realm of emotions, art, or relationships.

The Legacy king holds his cup carefully with both hands and gazes into the water, representing the focus of both his thoughts (his gaze) and his actions (his hands). The cup and water symbolize his heart and his dreams.

The Shadowscapes king surrounds himself with creatures who understand the flow of water—sea horses and turtles. He identifies with these unique creatures, for he, too, knows the currents of emotions and the power of dreams. He understands and makes good use of them.

King of Swords

The King of Swords both rules and is ruled by reason and logic. He delights in truth, enjoys communication, and finds comfort in clearly defined rules. The conviction that he is doing what is right drives him more than anything else. Hence, we often find him in the government. He may also practice or enforce the law, be a scientist, do medical research, perform surgery, or work in media. When approaching the King of Swords, check all emotional pleas at the door; don't expect excitement or passion to sway him. Focus on reason and logic, having all the points clearly defined, and express them as simply and elegantly as possible. If you digress too much, you'll lose his attention.

KING of SWORDS.

King of Swords

King of Swords

The Universal Waite king sees himself as the wielder of the sword of truth and all that is right and just. His experience makes him capable of making sound decisions.

Core meaning:
One who has authority, makes decisions, or is a professional in the realm of ideas, systems, or communication.

The Legacy king stands between two pillars surrounded by symbols of wings and clouds, representing his dedication to higher thought and wisdom. He holds his sword down, indicating the application of his decisions in the world.

The Shadowscapes card shows that this king believes that physical man, as represented by the Leonardo da Vinci figure, is subordinate to the realms of the mind. A man who keeps himself low is guided by crows; a man who raises himself to loftier heights, taking in the whole picture, receives the wisdom of the owl.

King of Pentacles

The King of Pentacles is practical and values results. He likes things to run efficiently and effectively while producing something of quality. He tends to move in financial circles, such as banking, investing, and real estate. Tangible goods also interest him, and he is an excellent salesperson. Because he values material goods, he might also work in protection or security. Finally, combining the desire for results and the physical world, coaching is a natural fit for him. Gaining his interest or support is easy if the querent can show him how her ideas will make his life easier or more productive. Focus on both the bottom line and good quality, and you'll find him an attentive listener.

KING of PENTACLES.

King of Coins

King of Pentacles

The Universal Waite king is entirely immersed in his prosperity. His garden seems a bit overgrown and he may look a little soft, but he is careful to reveal the armor under his robes.

Core meaning:
One who has authority, makes decisions, or is a professional in the realm of the physical world, resources, or finances.

The Legacy king gazes from his balcony as if the world were his oyster, which it probably is. He has plenty and continues to seek ways to gain more.

The Shadowscapes king embodies the stability and power of the earth combined with the strength and drive of a dragon. He has the ability to see abundance in ways others do not, as symbolized by the acorn by his hand.

3: Finding More Meaning

Remember way back in the beginning when I said that learning tarot was like learning to read? Words and simple sentences are the beginning of communication. But other things—punctuation, sentence structure, word choice—lend nuance and precision to whatever you speak or write. It is the same with interpreting tarot cards. The cards have core meanings, but by applying more techniques, you can add layers and depth to your readings.

In chapter 1, we discussed the options of turning the cards over all at once or one by one. A benefit of turning them over all at once is being able to scan the reading for themes indicated by card types, numbers, or suits. For example, if you see a high proportion of Major Arcana cards (more than one third) in the reading, you know that this reading is particularly significant, with spiritual importance, and showing that at least some of the situation is out of the querent's control. Scanning the reading is a useful way to create the background for the interpretation of the spread. By looking at the number, suits, and combinations of cards, you can gain extra insight that will help shape the core meanings into a full and precise interpretation.

Numbers

Many times, people want to know when something is going to happen or when a situation will resolve itself. Timing is a tricky thing, and most readers have their own ways of handling timing questions. One is to build the issue of timing into the question, such as "What can I expect in terms of my love life in the next three months?" Another is to scan the reading and use the numbers to indicate where the situation is in its development. If there are multiples of a certain range of numbers, that lets you know where the situation is. For example:

> **Aces–Threes:** the situation is just beginning or in the early stages.
>
> **Fours–Sixes:** the situation is in the middle.
>
> **Sevens–Nines:** the situation is nearing the end.
>
> **Tens:** the situation is all but over.

When considering the idea of free will and how much we can affect our futures, looking at the numbers in this way can be helpful in determining how much influence we can exert. In the beginning of a situation, it is easier to create change with less effort. The closer a situation gets to resolution, the more challenging it is and the more effort is required. Here is an example. When you first start dating someone, you can more easily change direction. That is, if you choose not to see the person anymore after a few dates (aces–threes), it is easy enough to say so, with few repercussions. However, if it is the night before the wedding (tens), while you can still say no, it will be harder and the ramifications larger.

Suits

The suits give important information about the situation as well. The suits, remember, are associated with elements: wands are fire, cups are water, swords are air, and pentacles are earth (see pages 21–22 and the sections on aces for more information). The elements are often visible on the cards in terms of symbolism or color, making it easy to see at a glance what elemental energies are involved. At the most basic level, you can observe the balance—or lack of balance—of energy in a situation. Many cups indicate an emotional situation, something you would not be surprised to see in a reading about a relationship but might not expect in a career reading. Noticing things like this can help you understand the basic situation from the querent's perspective. If your querent asks about their career and more cups show up than wands or pentacles, the querent is probably more interested in creative work or work that satisfies their soul than a fast-track career path or even money.

The suits and the elemental energy they represent can be used in another way as well. Using the suits can also help determine the ease or difficulty in controlling a situation. It is rare that a reading contains only one suit. Usually there are several, if not all, of the suits present. This means there is more than one type of energy present in the situation. There is nothing unusual in that; most situations have several aspects. Understanding how the elemental energies affect each other can give us an idea of the conflicts or harmony in the situation. Here are how the elements affect each other:

- Cards of the same element strengthen each other greatly.

- Wands (fire) and swords (air) are both considered active and support each other.
- Cups (water) and pentacles (earth) are both considered passive and support each other.

- Wands (fire) and cups (water) are opposites and weaken each other.
- Swords (air) and pentacles (earth) are opposites and weaken each other.

- Wands (fire) and pentacles (earth) have little effect on each other.
- Swords (air) and cups (water) have little effect on each other.

When an element is strengthened, it does not always mean that it is a positive situation. It means that the experience is stronger or intensified, whether positive or negative.

Fire and air are considered active. This means the energy is active—it moves, it creates, it acts; it also indicates swift movement. That is, if this energy is present, it is moving around, making things happen and happen quickly.

Water and earth are considered passive. That is, the energy is passive, it is still, it is reactive, it is shaped; it also suggests slower movement. Passive energy waits for something to happen—hence the idea of slowness—and then reacts.

When either water and fire or air and earth are present, the result is a weakening of both. They are opposites, fighting against each other, causing conflicting energy that will be evidenced in the situation.

The combinations of fire and earth or air and water are considered neutral. They have little or no effect on each other.

Scanning a spread and paying attention to numbers and suits can be a useful way to understand the state of a situation before interpreting the individual cards. Scanning creates a background, then each card in the spread adds details until finally you have a whole picture before you.

Elemental Dignities

Many readers use a technique called elemental dignities. This is different than scanning a spread, but it is similar in that it uses the same elemental relationships listed on the opposite page. Instead of scanning the reading as a whole, when applying elemental dignities, we look at whatever card we are interpreting. We consider the cards that are next to or above or below it. Using the elemental relationships, we consider the effect on the particular card we are looking at.

For example, let's say we are looking at the Three of Cups (core meaning: a spontaneous, unexpected joy or pleasure). Next to it is the Five of Wands. Technically, it doesn't matter if it is five or any other number; what matters is the suit. In this case, it is wands, or fire. Wands/fire is the opposite of cups/water, therefore weakening the card. The spontaneous joy or pleasure will not be quite as joyful or pleasurable as it could be; it is weakened, or diminished, by the presence of wands/fire.

One way to think about elemental dignities is to think of a card as a word and the card next to it as a modifier. The modifier can indicate an intensification of meaning, like underlining or adding an exclamation point does in writing. A modifier can also diminish the impact by adding "kind of" or "meh" to the sentence.

Using elemental relationships, whether in scanning or in dignities, is easiest and least confusing when just applied to the Minor Arcana. However, many people do include the Major Arcana, associating each of those cards with a different element. I have not discovered a system of Major Arcana elemental association that seems at all elegant or sensible, so I do not use one at all. Using the elemental energy of the Minor Arcana will work very well, at least to start. Later, you can decide for yourself about the Major Arcana.

For more information on elemental dignities, see Paul Hughes-Barlow's site: http://supertarot.co.uk.

Reversals

Just as elemental dignities can affect a card's interpretation, so can the use of reversals. Reversals are when a card appears upside down in a spread. Here's a card upright and reversed:

In the early days of fortunetelling, reversed meanings were always used in readings, as far as I know. If you look in older books on interpreting the cards, you will notice that sometimes the reversed meaning was the direct opposite of the upright meaning or something altogether different. Here is an example of traditional upright and reversed meanings for the Two of Swords:

> **Upright:** balanced forces, stalemate, indecision, impotence, a temporary truce in family quarrels.
>
> **Reversed:** release; movement of affairs, sometimes in the wrong direction. Caution against dealings with rogues.

I suppose it is always good advice to use caution when dealing with rogues, whether or not the Two of Swords shows up reversed. This example is not unusual. In the past—and even now, to some extent—the idea of a reversed card didn't or doesn't always have consistency. There often seems to be no relationship between the upright and reversed meanings. Modern tarotists have addressed this issue and devised various solutions to the problem. Readers look for a system that makes sense and has consistency. For example: all reversals mean the exact opposite of the upright meaning. Or, all reversals mean the same as the upright meaning, simply weakened, delayed, or blocked. Or special attention should be paid to that card. One popular system is simply not to use reversals. If a card is upside down in the spread, simply turn it right-side up and continue on with the reading. There are many readers who use this method, or non-method. For a beginner, I would suggest not using reversals for a while. However, if you are interested in employing reversals, check out Mary K. Greer's *Complete Book of Tarot Reversals*, where she presents an intelligent discussion of reversals and various systems to try for yourself.

Significators

We'll close this section with one more technique: the use of significators. Back in the fortunetelling days, significators were selected a few different ways. An early method was to always use the High Priestess for a female querent and the Magician for a male querent. The significator card was placed at the top of the reading to simply represent the querent. It was not used in any other way; all it really accomplished was to take one card from the deck out of play. Later, readers used the court cards as significators, making the selection based on physical appearance, astrological sign, age, gender, or personality traits. (If you are interested, see appendix C for significator bullet points.) Again, the cards were set aside or placed in the spread but not interpreted. Again, they simply represented the querent but served no other purpose save for removing a card from play. There are other ways to use significator cards that are more useful.

If you are using a spread that has a position designated "significator," do not select a card for that spot. Instead, shuffle as you usually would and simply deal the cards. Whatever card turns up in that spot serves as the significator and can be interpreted as usual for the position, meaning it represents the querent in this situation.

Another way to incorporate a significator is to select a card for the querent based on appearance, astrological sign, etc. Include the selected card in the reading, and use it with the scanning technique or in elemental dignities. In this way, it plays an actual role in the reading.

Finally, if the querent's question involves someone else, you can determine ahead of time what cards will represent the querent and the other person (or people). Leave the cards in the deck, and shuffle as usual. If the cards show up in the spread, read them as representing the people indicated. I must mention here that reading for third parties is a matter of contention among modern tarotists. Some maintain that it is unethical to read about someone without their permission, that it is an invasion of privacy, or that it is not healthy for the querent, who should focus on their own issues, not someone else's actions. There are also those who think that it is not a problem—that people discuss others all the time with friends, family, counselors, therapists, and clergy. This is a question that every reader must decide: will you read for third parties or not?

Deciding whether or not to use significators, to read for third parties, or to flip all the cards over one by one are just a few decisions tarot readers have to make. Think about these possibilities, write about your ideas in your journals, try them out in your readings. Determining these issues, and others, will help you create your own style and direct your practice. The issues we explored in this chapter focused mostly on incorporating information from the cards into your interpretations, practices that directly affect your readings. In the next chapter, we'll explore some ideas that are not specifically related to interpreting the cards but can still directly affect your readings.

4: Adding Something Extra

As we discussed in chapter 1, ritual plays an important role in a tarot reading. The ritual (or rituals) need not be elaborate or dramatic to be useful. It simply needs to be repeated each time a reading is performed and to be an action that brings you to a place of peaceful focus. Simplicity can be a beautiful thing, creating a calm, Zen-like atmosphere. And many modern tarotists do prefer to avoid the Gypsy fortuneteller stereotype at all costs. However, we should be careful not to throw the baby out with the bathwater. There is something to be said in favor of an over-the-top sensual mystical experience.

When I was in college, I did a reading for an acquaintance who stopped by. Another friend and fellow medieval history student, Rob, observed the reading (with the querent's permission). At the time, my readings were very simple and eschewed anything mystical or Gypsy-like. After the querent left, Rob said, "You should add a little sense of ritual and drama to your readings. You know how important a sense of experience is in helping people accept wisdom. Even if it is just psychological, you're helping them receive the message. Isn't that what you are supposed to do?"

Rob had a point, but it is a sticky wicket for modern tarotists. We don't want to be viewed as charlatans, cold readers, scam artists, or crazy. Most readers want to be viewed as professionals and so are careful to present themselves as such. How much drama and mystery to add to a reading is something each reader must decide. And there is not just the idea of adding drama for drama's sake; we should take into account our beliefs as well.

Now we will consider a few techniques and practices that are fairly common.

Sacred Space

Pagans will be familiar with the idea of sacred space and the ritual of casting a circle. A tarot reading doesn't require a magical circle (although if you are so inclined, it doesn't hurt); however, many readers like to create the sense of being in a special place. A cloth or scarf is a portable and quick way to create an instant space. It defines the space to lay out the cards and becomes a focal point, causing everything else to recede into the background. This can be very helpful if you are reading in a public place with other potentially distracting activity going on around you. The cloth can be of any material, although traditionally silk was favored, especially if used to wrap the cards in afterwards, because it is said to energetically protect the cards from undesirable vibrations. More important than the material, however, is the color and pattern. The cards should always be the focus and the cloth nothing more than background, so select a color and pattern that enhance but do not clash with your cards. A cloth of velvet or cotton helps the cards stay in place; cards may slide around or be difficult to pick up on a silky fabric or satin cloth.

Many readers like to include items that represent the tarot's elemental energies. A stone, crystal, pentacle, bowl of salt, or a little soil can represent pentacles/earth. A glass of water or a seashell can indicate cups/water. A candle is the most common symbol for wands/fire, although an actual wand or twig can be used as well. Swords/air is present in the form of incense or a feather, or a small knife, or athame, for a more literal representation. Depending on your belief system, you can get as detailed as you like with your symbols. You can pick a crystal based on its healing or divinatory properties, such as tiger's-eye; an incense that promotes psychic abilities, such as frankincense; and candle colors for specific ideals, such as white to represent purity or purple to represent spirituality and higher wisdom.

People who have a knack for creating great experiences know that all the senses should be involved. Sight is easy: there are the cards themselves plus whatever else is included in your reading space. Scented candles or incense engage the sense of smell. Some readers rub essential oil into their hands and then hold their tarot deck, rubbing the oil into the edges of cards so they pick up the scent. Playing soft music in the background, ringing a small bell at the beginning of the reading, or regulating your voice bring in pleasing sounds. As for the sense of touch, there is a product called fanning powder used by stage magicians to keep their cards from sticking. Fanning powder is applied to the cards and makes them feel wonderful. It takes some time to apply, because you have to cover and then wipe off each card individually, but it is worth the effort and really enhances the feel of any deck in your hands and whoever else touches or shuffles your deck. Finally, there is the sense of taste, which can be pleased by sharing with your querent a simple beverage, cookie, chocolate, or piece of fruit. Keep it simple and small—and clean; no one wants food smudges all over their cards.

Finales

Many memorable events end with a grand finale, kind of like dessert. While it is hard to imagine exactly what a full-blown tarot finale might be, we can still end our readings with something special. The following practices have several benefits. First, they provide something concrete that can be taken away from the reading. Second, if you are reading for a querent, they help signal to the querent that the reading is drawing to a close. As you are ready to close the reading, you can:

- Ask one final question and draw one card as the answer.
- Draw one card for one piece (or one more piece) of advice regarding the situation.
- Draw one card and use it to create an affirmation.
- Draw one card for a special message from the Divine.

For this final card, you can use the same deck you used for the reading or you can use a different deck entirely. You can use another deck but only draw from the Major Arcana. You can use an oracle deck; oracle decks are similar to tarot decks in that they are used for divination or inspiration. However, they do not follow the structure of a tarot deck. Many readers prefer a tarot deck for most questions but do like the variety of using an oracle deck as part of the reading. With the wide variety of decks available, it would be easy to find one that either appeals to you or complements your tarot deck (in art style or theme), or both.

Even after the actual reading is over, there still may be some loose ends to tie up. Just as we signaled our minds that a reading was about to begin, we should also bring a sense of closure when the reading is over. Just one or a series of small rituals can be used. Here are some examples of simple actions that can be used as closing rituals:

- Blowing out a candle.
- Ringing a bell.
- Gathering the cards into a pile and tapping the pile three times with your index finger.
- Putting the cards away in a box or bag or wrapping them in a cloth.
- Closing your eyes and taking three deep breaths.
- Centering and grounding.
- Saying a prayer or blessing.
- Eating something grounding, such as a piece of chocolate or bread.

Cleansing and Storing Your Cards

Some readers, particularly those who are very sensitive to the energy around them, ritually cleanse their cards before or after every use. A very simple way to do this is to go through all the cards and make sure they are upright, and then put them in order (for example, in the same order as they are presented in this book, or the same order but putting the court cards with their suits). Nothing fancy—it is merely a way to signal to your mind that you are done reading the cards and that everything is in order until the next time. Another easy technique is to hold all the cards in your hand, fanned out, and just wave them through the air, imagining any residual energy falling off the cards. One of my favorite ideas is from Rachel Pollack, who suggests that after reading, which creates a certain kind of order, we "return our cards to their original state of chaos by shuffling after a reading."

Although still fairly simple, more elaborate techniques include burning sage or an incense with cleansing properties and passing the cards, as a deck or each card individually, through the smoke. A benefit of storing your cards in a bag or container with extra room is that you can include a crystal or stone. Rose quartz, obsidian, or tiger's-eye are popular choices, but use any stone that has properties that you like or want to incorporate into your readings. Other items can be stored with your cards, too, such as a sprig of sage or lavender, a rune stone, or any other talisman.

At the very least, after you are done using your cards, you'll want to gather them up and store them in something so that none of the cards get lost and so that they all stay clean and dry.

Keeping your cards safe and being able to wrap up a reading are practical benefits of rituals. Other benefits are less tangible but still very powerful. As with spirituality, ritual can be very personal. As with deciding what kind of questions you will ask, you will need to decide for yourself what, if any, ritual practices you want to incorporate.

While you are mulling over your options, we can shift our attention back to reading the cards with some hands-on activities and methods for adding nuance and precision to your readings.

5: Developing Your Skills

Some books suggest that you sleep with your tarot deck under your pillow in order to bond with it. Having never tried it, I cannot recommend the practice. However, I do believe that a good tarot reader develops a relationship with their cards far beyond simply learning basic core meanings. Think of it this way: almost anyone can go to cosmetology school and train to be a hair stylist. All the graduates, in theory, can cut hair. But there are always some whose work seems a little bit better, more pulled together and polished. Then there are some who seem like artists that work with hair. It is the same with many skills, and it is the same with tarot. Almost anyone can learn to read the cards with minimal effort. With practice, experimentation, and attention, almost anyone can become a very good reader.

In order to improve your reading skills, the very least you need to do is practice reading the cards. Learning the meanings is like learning your ABCs. You can recite them; you can use your tarot cards like flashcards. But that is just the first step. When you put the letters together and make words—or combine cards to create a reading—that's when the magic happens.

Take every opportunity to shuffle your cards. Get used to how they feel in your hands. Lay them out. Create words, make music, discover magic. Read for yourself. Read for friends and family. Read for your dog or cat. Pretend to read for celebrities or imaginary people. Join a tarot forum online and exchange readings with others.

By practicing, you'll start learning how the cards—*your* cards—work together with each other and with you. You'll learn how you interpret the cards, which may turn out to be different from the meanings given in this book. You'll learn nuances, and cards that seemed so similar at first will reveal their differences. If you really want to dig into developing your own meanings and forming your own relationship with the cards, work through Mary K. Greer's *21 Ways to Read a Tarot Card*. It takes the reader on a journey that creatively reveals hidden depths of wisdom.

Experimenting with Your Cards

Practicing basic readings will go a long way in helping you develop your relationship with your cards. You can advance this relationship by experimenting with your cards. Experimenting is like studying but usually more fun and more hands-on. Most of the following experiments are designed to help you understand how the cards each mean something different; they are unique. Understanding the differences between the cards is an important exercise, not only because it makes us more precise and accurate readers but also because it helps us maintain objectivity. Objectivity is important … and also difficult, especially when reading for ourselves or someone we care very much about, or in a situation about which we have a very strong opinion.

Experiment 1: What's the Difference?

Go through your deck and select cards that seem similar to you. For example, the four aces; the four kings (or any other court card); the Tower, the Wheel, and Death; the Ten of Wands and Ten of Swords; the Two of Wands and the Three of Wands; or the Two of Cups, Ten of Cups, and Ten of Pentacles. Consider all the ways in which the cards are the same. How are their meanings similar? More importantly, how are they different? Use a single question and interpret each of the cards you selected in turn as the answer. To learn more about the differences between seemingly similar cards, check out Kim Huggens' *Tarot 101*. Instead of presenting the Major Arcana in numerical order, she groups them according to similarity of theme.

Experiment 2: Reverse Reading

Ask a question. Think of the answer that you want. Go through your cards face-up and select a card for each position to create that perfect answer. Take your time. If necessary, lay out two or three cards for each position and consider each until you make a final decision. Ask yourself why you chose the cards you did. If you hesitated between two or more cards, what convinced you to pick the card you finally did? How was that card different than the other? How would the reading be different if you picked the other card instead? If you didn't have trouble selecting between cards, go through the deck and swap out a card or two for ones that are similar, and notice how that changes the answer.

Experiment 3: What Didn't Show Up?

When you are doing a reading, take some time to think about what cards didn't show up, and ask yourself why. For example, let's say you do a reading and the Three of Swords shows up. Ask, why that card instead of the Ten of Swords or Death? If you are doing a reading about a relationship, wondering if marriage is in your future, what would you think about a reading that *didn't* include the Ten of Cups, Ten of Pentacles, Four of Wands, or Hierophant (all cards associated with marriage)? What if, instead, there were the Two of Cups, Three of Cups, and the Eight of Wands?

Experiment 4: Context Is Everything

A tarot reading is an answer to a question, whether that question is verbalized or not. An important part of the art of reading is interpreting the cards so that they form an answer that makes sense. If someone asks, "What color is that apple?" and the other person answers, "Triangle," we would think that is not a useful answer. If a querent asks, "Is there anything exciting coming up in my romantic life?" and the Queen of Cups comes up, we will not recite the core meaning of "one who develops and cares for others in the realm of emotions, art, or relationships." Instead, we shape that core into something that makes sense and is relevant to the question. Since this card represents someone interested in helping the querent in the realm of relationships, I'd say the answer is yes, something exciting *is* likely coming up—that there is someone coming into (or already in) the querent's life who will help the querent find romance.

To practice shaping the core meanings into relevant answers, make a list of questions. Then pull one card and use it to form an answer for all the questions you listed.

Here are a few sample questions to get you started:

- Should I _____ (fill in the blank: get a new job, dump my boyfriend, date so-and-so, move to Paris)?
- What will happen regarding _____ (fill in the blank: my love life, my family, my career, my living situation)?
- How can I _____ (fill in the blank: make more money, find love, find peace, find a good place to live, figure out what I want)?
- Where should I go for vacation this year?
- I need a new look…what should I do?
- I have writer's/artist's block. What should I write about/ paint/create?
- My _____ (fill in the blank: mother, sister, boy-friend, boss, coworker, client) is driving me crazy. What can I do?

Spread positions are very similar to questions; in fact, some are actual questions (see chapter 6). Here is another way to practice shaping core meanings based on a technique I learned from James Wells. Select a spread that you like. Again, pull a single card. Interpret that card in each position in the spread.

Add to this experiment by reading pairs of cards (or even groups of three) instead of single cards. Blending the question, the core meanings, and elemental dignities, what kinds of answers do you get? How does using more cards confuse or clarify the interpretation for you? As you become more comfortable with reading the cards as parts of a larger answer, you will become quicker and more confident.

Experiment 5: Presentation Is Everything

We've discussed objectivity and the idea of including our own judgments and opinions in the card meanings. This exercise helps you practice paying attention to how a card can be presented in a favorable, neutral, or negative manner. Pull a card and talk about it in three different ways. First, as a neutral communicator of information. Second, as someone who thinks this card is absolutely wonderful or who at least takes an optimistic view of it. Third, read the card as a very negative message or as a pessimist. Try this with several cards, including ones that you think of as being either positive or negative.

Remember, learning to read the cards is like learning to read. Start with thinking of the cards as the alphabet and continually build your skills, beginning with simple words and then moving on to simple sentences. Eventually you will become adept at more complex sentences, continually increase your vocabulary, and master subtle nuances of meaning and inflection.

Multiples and Combinations

Learning individual cards is important, as is learning how cards react with each other to create complex and unique answers. In chapter 3, we also discussed the idea of scanning the cards in a reading to create a background for the card-by-card interpretation. In scanning a reading, we noticed how cards worked together to create patterns using numbers and suits to provide additional information about the situation. We learned that multiples of certain card ranges give clues about timing. There are other multiples that can bring meaning to a reading as well, so keep your eyes peeled for two or more cards having the same number or rank; they add emphasis to a reading.

Aces: a window of opportunity that won't last long

Twos: a decision

Fours: a stable or stagnant situation

Fives: conflict

Pages: a message

Knights: things are moving quickly

In addition to multiples of cards, many readers rely on recognizing pairs of cards or combinations of cards to relay certain information. The two or three cards together emphasize, narrow, or validate a certain meaning. An Empress card, based on the core meaning "abundance and creation" coupled with the picture of a pregnant woman, can be read as "pregnancy." However, the Empress can represent other aspects of creation besides giving birth. The Ace of Wands, an active, masculine card often with a phallic symbol on the card, helps focus the meaning of the Empress, indicating for many readers an actual pregnancy. But memorizing pairs can be tedious work. Instead of tackling a long list of pairs—indeed, there have been entire books written about tarot card combinations—focus on a few that make sense and build from there. Again, thinking of tarot reading like learning to read, it takes time to build a vocabulary. Below are some commonly used combinations:

- The Empress and Ace of Wands: pregnancy
- Seven of Cups and Two of Swords: unable to make a decision

- Eight of Wands and any knight(s): fast-moving events
- Any ace with any page: an opportunity
- The Chariot with any knight: travel
- Six of Swords and the Chariot: moving
- The Chariot and the World, Six of Wands, or any king: success
- Three of Cups or Nine of Cups and the Devil: drinking too much (alcohol)
- Eight of Swords or Ten of Swords and the Devil: self-created drama, playing the victim
- Ten of Swords and the Hanged Man: a sacrifice for the greater good
- Lovers, Ten of Cups, Hierophant, or Four of Wands: marriage
- The Magician and a court card with the Devil or the Moon: a deceptive or manipulative person

These are just a few tried and true combinations. Every reader eventually develops their own list based on their experience. Remember that any of these secondary techniques used in scanning are meant to support or verify the actual reading by creating a background. Let the actual cards and their meanings take precedence and supply the details and specifics of a reading.

Intuition

Amongst practitioners of both the psychic and the intuitive arts, there is much debate about the definitions of each of those terms. The discussions usually focus on how "psychic" and "intuitive" are different, and where, exactly, the information gleaned by these practices comes from. For this book, though, let's quiet the debate and accept the fact that all such wisdom comes from the Divine; whether the Divine is located outside of you or inside of you is not important right now. We'll use the words interchangeably and consider them to mean "a non-rational means of obtaining information, understanding, or wisdom."

Belief in psychic abilities is unnecessary for reading tarot cards. Like so many aspects of tarot reading, this is something every reader must decide about for themselves. If you don't believe in or don't have any interest in psychic techniques, skip this section. However, if the world of psychic powers interests you, then definitely explore it and see how it can fit into your practice. Many psychic readers use the cards as a springboard for their readings, and many readers use psychic practices to enhance their readings, but you don't have to consider yourself a psychic to do so. In fact, many readers are uncomfortable with calling themselves psychics and prefer the word "intuitive."

There are some very simple ways to invite psychic information or open your intuition. We've talked before about centering and grounding. That is useful for preparing for psychic work, too. By centering, we pull our energy into the core of our being so that we can focus and be fully present. By grounding, we connect to the earth and to the universe and to the Divine in a conscious and deliberate way, inviting wisdom to flow through us. As we calm our mind by centering and connect to the Divine by grounding, we are perfectly poised to receive intuitive insight.

But how, exactly, do we receive this insight in tarot reading? When scanning the spread, a symbol or pattern may catch our eye. Stopping to consider it, we feel that we know the meaning, even if it isn't necessarily an interpretation we'd usually apply to that symbol, card, or pattern. That is the most common way that intuition influences tarot readings: simply by presenting a different interpretation than we'd usually use. Most readers call these experiences "intuitive hits." They come to recognize certain sensations that accompany their hits, such as a visual, audible, or even olfactory experience, an emotional reaction, or a deep conviction that they "just know" something is true.

Just centering, grounding, and being open to receiving intuitive information can add layers of insight, meanings, and relevance to your readings. As with any practice, there is always more to learn. If you are interested in psychic tarot readings, do read Nancy Antenucci and Melanie Howard's *Psychic Tarot*. In the meantime, here are two more methods to enhance the reception of psychic or intuitive information that work for many readers.

Ask

Specifically ask the Divine, your Higher Self, or the universe to strengthen your connection; to guide you; to help you hear or see intuitive information; and to relay it to the querent for her greater good. When you ask, be prepared for whatever will come; let go of expectations; trust the insight you receive. When working intuitively, trust is very important. We are listening to a voice or sensing information from a source we cannot easily identify or explain, which makes the logical mind a little crazy. The logical mind will likely tell us we are nuts. The logical mind can be very persuasive. With intuition, we don't have proof that will satisfy the mind, so we must have faith.

Connect with Your Querent

If we believe that all the answers to all the questions we have can be found within, then the job of the reader is to help the querent hear their own answers. Connecting with your querent is a way of asking her Higher Self to talk to your Higher Self, so you can provide the needed wisdom. I prefer this method that I learned from Geraldine Amaral. First, ask your querent for permission to connect with her Higher Self. Have your querent place her hands in front of you, palms up. Place your hands over your querent's hands with your palms down, palms touching lightly. Close your eyes, breathe, and focus on your querent. Tune in to your Higher Self as it talks to your querent's Higher Self. Ask it to guide you during the reading. As you move your hands to continue with the reading, ask that the connection remain intact until the reading is completed. Afterwards, thank both your Higher Self and your querent's Higher Self for their assistance and guidance.

Experiment with accessing psychic or intuitive information. While it is impossible to supply a logical explanation for intuitive hits, it is possible to build confidence to help bolster trust in them. The simplest and most common way to do this is to keep track of your intuitive or psychic experiences. Note the details of the reading, what techniques you employed, what you sensed or experienced, what you said, and how the querent reacted. If possible, follow up with the querent to see how the information played out in their lives.

Intuition is considered an important element in tarot readings by many people. If incorporating intuition in your tarot practice doesn't work for you, don't worry about it. It is not a prerequisite to being a good reader. Scanning a spread, working with elements and numbers, and using elemental dignities or combinations are not mandatory either. Try them all, but select the ones that work with your beliefs and that make sense to you. While you may not ultimately work with all these techniques, you will likely work with a few so that your readings flow together better and provide useful information. In addition to interpretation techniques, you get to decide which spread or spreads you like. Let's take a look at a few.

6: Spreads

Spreads are the framework for any reading. They provide shape and structure for the interpretation and ultimate answer or advice given to the querent. Tarot readers all have their own opinions about what makes a good spread, how many cards are ideal, how many spreads a reader should be familiar with, or even whether or not an actual spread should be used. As with anything related to tarot, try out as many options as possible before making a decision. Most teachers encourage students to start with smaller spreads, such as one to three cards. I think three-card readings are the best to start with, because three cards provide enough material to work with and allow the reader to practice using some of the techniques taught in this book. One-card readings can be very, very insightful, especially for readers who are quite intuitive and love finding meanings in their cards that go beyond core meanings.

One-Card Spread

Sometimes less is more. There is a simple clarity to a one-card answer. Conversely, if it is true that a picture is worth a thousand words, then it is possible to find great depth and wisdom in just one card. And the beauty of this "spread" is that it can be used to answer almost any question. Simply ask the question and draw one card. For example:

- What do I need to know today?
- What should I give my sister for her birthday?
- Should I go to the party tonight or stay home and read?
- How can I earn more money?
- Why am I feeling this way?

Three-Card Readings

As you know from your experiments in chapter 5, three cards working together create complex and unique answers. For some readers, one card just isn't enough to work with. Use the idea from the one-card spread—that is, ask a single question—and draw three cards instead of one for the answer.

Most people start off with three-card readings that have positional meanings (as opposed to using three cards to answer one question, described above). These readings allow for more complex, or multifaceted, questions and enable us to see relationships between aspects of a situation. Three-card readings are very flexible and can be easily adapted to almost any question. Try some of these or invent your own.

1: Past	Present	Future
2: The Situation	The Problem	The Solution
3: The Decision	Choice 1	Choice 2
4: The Situation	What To Do	What Not To Do
5: The Situation	Challenge	Advice

Celtic Cross Spread

The Celtic Cross Spread is a very traditional and well-known spread, included in almost every tarot book for beginners. There are many reasons it is so well known and popular. It provides a wealth of information about any situation. There are enough cards to provide plenty of material to work with. It gives a clear overview of a situation as well as the probable outcome. It can be read as a large spread or as a series of smaller spreads. Because the Celtic Cross Spread has been around for about one hundred years (it was invented by Arthur E. Waite, who falsely claimed it was an ancient spread), there are many variations. You may see versions that label the positions slightly differently. Remember, tarot has evolved and continues to evolve, and that goes for spreads, too. It's okay. Don't assume that one variation is wrong and the other, right. In addition to a variety of positional meanings, people have altered or added to the Celtic Cross layout. As you work with it, if you notice areas or types of information that you'd like, add positions and see how they work out.

In chapter 4, we talked about the importance of creating an experience during a reading. The Celtic Cross, as first presented by A. E. Waite, included instructions for a dramatic presentation. The reader was told to lay down the significator, saying it represented the querent. When laying down the first card, the reader must say, "This card covers her." With the next, "This card crosses her." For the third, "This card crowns her"; for the next, "This card is the foundation," and so on. The words don't really mean anything, but said in the right way, they certainly can add a sense of style to a reading.

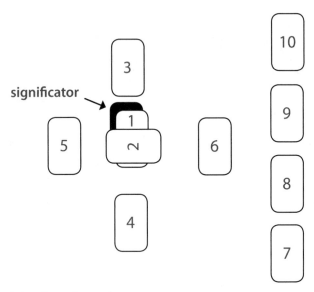

Celtic Cross Spread

Significator

1. **Covers:** the influence that is affecting the querent or the situation

2. **Crosses:** the obstacles or energies working against the querent in this situation

3. **Crown:** the querent's ideal, or goal, in the situation

4. **Foundation:** the basis, or foundation, of the situation

5. **Behind:** influences that affected the querent or situation but are now passing away

6. **Before:** what is likely to happen next

7. **Yourself:** the querent as she sees herself in the situation

8. **Your House:** the influences of circumstances or people surrounding the querent

9. **Hopes and Fears:** the querent's hopes and/or fears regarding this situation

10. **What Will Come:** the culmination, resolution, or outcome of the situation

This spread was originally designed for purely predictive readings, and the position meanings show that. For this, or any spread you try, always tweak the meanings so that they make sense with your beliefs and your reading style. For example, if you do not like how "the culmination, resolution, or outcome of the situation" implies a sense of absolute, written-in-stone fate, change it to something like "the current most likely outcome if all things remain as they are." If the outcome isn't to the querent's liking, a common practice is to follow up with another short one- to three-card reading to advise the querent about how to change that outcome.

As mentioned earlier, the Celtic Cross can be read as several mini spreads as well as one large one. For example, the first mini spread is the cross in the center made up of the significator, the covering card, and the crossing card. These cards, read together, very concisely create a picture of the situation or conflict concerning the querent. Card 5, the significator, and card 6 together make the familiar three-card spread of past-present-future. Cards 6 and 10 show the trend of future events. Cards 3 and 9 tell what the querent wants, hopes for, or fears. Reading these cards in these combinations also allows you to use your skills in reading card pairs and elemental dignities to add nuances to the reading.

Life Spread

One of my very favorite spreads is the Life Spread developed and taught by Josephine Ellershaw. Josephine wrote the *Easy Tarot Handbook* and *Easy Tarot Reading* (which will be available fall 2011). Both books are wonderful, but you will probably, at this point in your practice, find *Easy Tarot Reading* to be more useful. It presents detailed instructions for readings, as well as sample readings. Josephine teaches using the Life Spread, along with another spread called the Anchor, which uses only the Major Arcana. This is most useful if you have two decks, so you can have both the Life Spread and the Anchor on the table at the same time. However, I've found that, especially for beginners, using just the Life Spread is quite useful and less overwhelming.

Beyond the key card, number 21, and the key cards for the groupings of home, career, personal, love, and future, there are no fixed meanings for the positions. The key cards for the groupings are the ones on top of the other three: 1, 5, 9, 13, and 17. These cards represent the most important influences in the grouping and should be used as the core that ties the other three cards together.

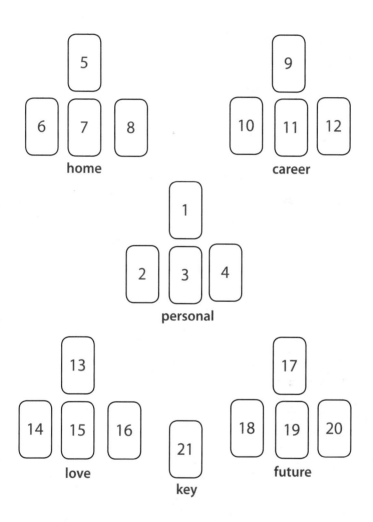

Life Spread

The one-card, three-card, Celtic Cross, and Life spreads should keep you busy for quite a while. Between all of them, with perhaps a little tweaking, you should be able to find a spread to answer any question. If you simply don't care for any of these—if they don't suit your purposes or you just want to try some new spreads—there are plenty of good books about spreads available, such as Teresa Michelsen's *Designing Your Own Tarot Spreads* and Sylvia Abraham's *How to Use Tarot Spreads*. And if you can wait until 2012, you can get *Tarot Spreads for Beginners*, the sequel to this book. In addition, the companion books that come with decks usually have several spreads that can work with any deck. And don't forget to check online. Tarot authors (such as Mary K. Greer—http://marygreer.wordpress.com/2008/04/05/the-hidden-influences-spread/), tarot blogs, and tarot forums often have spreads available.

Now that we've looked at the cards, their meanings, interpretation techniques, and spreads, maybe we should watch over the shoulder of a reader and see one way all of this can be put together.

7: Sample Readings

With something as personal as tarot reading, it is difficult to determine if sample readings will be helpful or not. Most teachers want to provide students with enough foundational information and framework so that they feel confident enough to jump in and try it themselves. This way, the students can feel free to find their own unique tarot-reading voice and develop their own style without being influenced by examples of how it is "supposed" to be done. On the other hand, when doing a tarot reading, there can be many elements to balance. Seeing how someone else does it can provide clarity and inspiration. You may choose to skip these examples entirely; that's perfectly fine. If you do read them, know that they are examples only. If a card in one of these readings is interpreted a certain way, it does not mean it always should be so or that any other way is wrong.

The following samples will include readings of various lengths and styles. For example, there will be predictive, prescriptive, interactive, and intuitive reading samples. One of the short readings will be done in each style to show how your approach affects a reading. It is an interesting experiment to try a reading for yourself in this manner, and it will not only help you try out different reading styles, it can also present different ways to look at your question or situation. In the end, you will likely develop a style that blends all four of these together in a unique way.

For this example, Sara, a twenty-nine-year-old woman, wants information about her love life. The reading will be a three-card spread with no positional meanings. The question will be phrased slightly differently for the four reading styles. The same cards will be used for each reading. Starting with a predictive reading, the question is: "What can Sara expect in the area of her love life in the next three months?"

Using the Universal Waite deck, the three cards drawn are the Two of Pentacles, Ace of Swords, and Two of Cups.

The ace and twos indicate that Sara is at the beginning of a new phase in her romantic life. The pair of twos emphasizes that there is a decision she must make that relates to this situation. The decision is probably between the Two of Pentacles and the Two of Cups, and being earth and water, they are pretty evenly weighted in her mind. The presence of air in the form of the Ace of Swords weakens the Two of Pentacles and has little effect on the Two of Cups, but here, that small effect will have big repercussions. The Two of Pentacles means maintaining balance. Sara has been living a stable and balanced life—so stable that she has become almost hypnotized by the rhythm of her Zen-like days. The Ace of Swords promises an opportunity for a new way of thinking—in this case, a new way of thinking about romance. By embracing this, she will shake up her Two of Pentacles trance and open up to the experience indicated by the Two of Cups, a deep emotional connection or attraction.

For the prescriptive reading, the question is: "What can Sara do to bring more love and romance into her life?"

The interpretation is very similar to the predictive reading, except instead of stating it as though this is what will happen, it is stated as advice. Sara has been focusing too much on trying to balance her life and on very practical things. She should look at her life in a new way and break her old patterns. Sara should focus on her emotions by paying attention to people or activities that attract her or that she feels connected to, and then she should respond to those emotions.

For the interactive reading, we will use the same question that we did for the prescriptive reading: "What can Sara do to bring more love and romance into her life?" Interactive readings are not necessarily either predictive or prescriptive; they simply involve the querent in the reading. This can be done in small ways, as in the example here. Other interactive techniques include involving the querent with the card interpretations on an intuitive level, by asking her what she sees in the cards and what that might mean to her.

Reader: Sara, the cards suggest that you are at the beginning of a new phase in your romantic life. Does that seem true to you?

Sara: Yes. About six months ago, I ended a relationship of about two years. I haven't been interested in dating since then, but now I feel ready to start.

Reader: The cards also suggest that there is a decision you need to make that is directly related to the question. Do you know what that decision is?

Sara: It could be about a guy I work with. It's not him but his brother, who I met when a group of people from work went out for happy hour. His brother came because they were going somewhere after. I was interested in him but can't decide if I should pursue it or not. I don't know if he is interested; I don't know if it could cause awkwardness at work.

Reader: The cards do show a fine balance between practical considerations and emotional ones. They are pretty evenly matched; however, there is a slight edge in favor of romance over practicality. So is your question really about pursuing this particular man?

Sara: Yes, that is mostly what I want to know.

Reader: Based on common sense, it is a close call, and the cards also support that conclusion. However, the appearance of the Two of Cups is a strong indication that the interest is mutual; this is always a positive, supportive card for questions about romance. The ace recommends a new way of thinking, a strong sense of decisiveness. Your choice is to contact him or not. If not, your life will go on as before: not bad, just stable. If you do contact him, there is potential and really very little sign of anything negative or dangerous. The ace, however, also says that the opportunity to act on this is short ... I'm not sure why, but the cards' advice is to act now. The Ace of Swords is also about truth and honesty—good advice when starting any new relationship.

For the intuitive reading, we'll use this question: "What does Sara need to know about her love life?" Intuitive readings are readings that use intuitive techniques. They are not necessarily predictive or prescriptive. Intuitive techniques can be used in both types. It is difficult to point out what in the cards triggers specific intuitive information. In this example, the reader connected with Sara, looked at the images, and began the reading.

Reader: Sara, the cards show that you have a choice to make. You are torn between practicality and emotion. You like stability and security; you value having good things now and planning for the future. You also dream of having a love that overwhelms you and fills your life. You think these things are mutually exclusive, that they are on opposite sides of possibility, but they are not. They are, or can be, two sides of the same coin ... not two different coins. A relationship is about giving and receiving: two sides. You need to understand that it is possible for a relationship to have both. By continuing to think it is one or the other, you keep yourself outside of love because of fear. It is good that you are thinking about this now, because there will be an opportunity very soon that will give you a chance to make this choice—not between practicality and love, but between being brave and being safe.

In this next example, Julie wants advice about her career. Things at work are fine, but she feels stagnant. She's been in the same position for about three years and feels it's time to either move up in the company or move on to somewhere else. For this reading, we'll use the Legacy of the Divine Tarot in a Celtic Cross. We will use a significator but let the deck determine the card randomly. To make things less complicated, we'll list the core meaning with the card name.

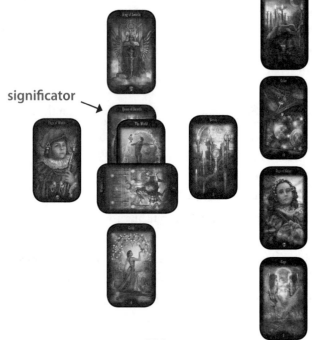

significator

Significator: Queen of Swords: One who develops and cares for others in the realm of ideas, systems, or communication.

1. **Covers:** The World: Successful completion.

2. **Crosses:** Six of Wands: Recognition of achievement.

3. **Crown:** King of Swords: One who has authority, makes decisions, or is a professional in the realm of ideas, systems, or communication.

4. **Foundation:** Nine of Coins: Accomplishment.

5. **Behind:** Page of Wands: One who observes in the realm of will, inspiration, or energy.

6. **Before:** Eight of Wands: Swift movement.

7. **Yourself:** Two of Cups: Deep emotional connection or attraction.

8. **Your House:** Page of Coins: One who observes in the realm of the physical world, resources, or finances.

9. **Hopes and Fears:** Ten of Coins: Stable and abundant life.

10. **What Will Come:** Nine of Wands: Preparing for the next challenge.

This is a pretty intense and fascinating spread, which makes perfect sense for someone as driven as Julie. Scanning the reading, the numbers indicate the end of a cycle, although it is interesting to note the two in the Yourself position—the situation is coming to an end, but Julie already sees herself as ready to begin anew. The end of the cycle idea is reinforced by the World as the covering card. There are four wands and three coins, showing the passion, drive, and commitment to succeed. Indeed, the World, the Six of Wands, the King and Queen of Swords, the Nine of Coins, and the Ten of Coins all reinforce the idea of success. Success is generally thought of as a very good thing, but it may not be in Julie's mind, at least not at this time. In fact, the success gives off a feeling of stagnation, of having been there and done that. It is being crossed by wands—by fire, by passion, by ambition, by the need for something new. None of this is really new to Julie, but it does provide an accurate backdrop for the reading.

Starting in the center of the reading, the Queen of Swords represents Julie, someone who loves to develop new ideas. She is covered by the World; she has successfully completed a phase of her career. She is crossed by the Six of Wands; her success is diminished because she wants to be recognized somehow for this achievement—as she stated, either by promotion within her company or by moving on.

Her highest goal is the King of Swords, someone with authority, clearly. The cards make a nice aesthetic point by saying she is the queen now but wishes to be king, the next level of advancement in the same suit.

The foundation of this situation is the Nine of Coins: accomplishment. How many times will the cards say this? Apparently it is important to recognize that the accomplishment, the success, is part of the problem here.

The Page of Wands is behind her. Court cards do often represent others in readings, but they also can represent the querent. In this case, it is easy to see that the first few court cards do represent Julie. In the past, she was the Page of Wands. She recognized what drove her, what inspired her. She knows that having achieved does not inspire her; the act of achieving is what she needs.

What is before her is the Eight of Wands, swift movement and, more specifically in the Legacy image, a calm before the storm. Things feel lined up and still, but something will come along to shake things up.

In this situation, Julie sees herself as someone attracted to something—in this case, the need for something more, a bigger, brighter new challenge. She has taken to this idea like someone falling in love. She is convinced that she must pursue it. She is almost giddy with the idea.

Her House is the Page of Coins, and in this case we should read the card as someone else, since the position explicitly states that it is other people. This person has something—an opportunity that they believe will grow into something big. This person holds potential. This card has coins and cups above and below it, so it is strengthened, adding to the idea that it is a positive opportunity. It is very likely that this person holds the key to what Julie needs.

Julie's hopes and fears are the Ten of Coins. She desires abundance as a way of measuring success, but she fears the stability that comes with it, as that dampens her drive.

The outcome card, the Nine of Wands, shows Julie literally preparing for the next challenge.

Julie wanted advice about her career, and the cards are giving her advice. To read the advice predictively, we would say that she should set her affairs in order as much as possible and be ready to react when something rather unexpected happens. It won't be entirely unexpected, as she is getting a reading that is preparing her to be on the lookout for it. The unexpected event will bring her into contact with someone who has an opportunity that will appeal to her. She is advised to take it and relish her time preparing for the new challenge. She will continue to succeed, but what she really wants is the challenge—the exhilaration of making something happen—and she will get that opportunity.

To read this more prescriptively, we might still say that she should arrange her affairs in such a way that she will be able to respond quickly to unexpected events. Then, instead of predicting that she will meet someone with an opportunity, we would advise her to seek out entrepreneurs with ideas and opportunities that she could become involved with.

In this example, Patricia wants a general reading about the state of her life. I'll use the Universal Waite and a freeform method of laying out the cards by placing them in three rows of three cards each and using no positional meanings. Although I assign no positions to start, they usually come up intuitively as the reading progresses.

> **Five of Cups:** Reactions to loss and grief.
>
> **Knight of Swords:** One who acts in the realm of ideas, systems, or communication.
>
> **Page of Swords:** One who observes in the realm of ideas, systems, or communication.
>
> **Two of Wands:** Gathering energy while refining your vision.
>
> **Six of Wands:** Recognition of achievement.
>
> **Three of Wands:** Active waiting.

Four of Swords: Respite from troubles.

Queen of Swords: One who develops and cares for others in the realm of ideas, systems, or communication.

Nine of Cups: Material, emotional, and physical well-being.

Even for a reader who wouldn't normally scan a spread, this one screams out to be scanned. Can anyone *not* notice the plethora of wands and swords? Clearly, Patricia's life is in a very active period. Wands and swords are active and fast-moving, so things are definitely happening. Most of the cards are in the early to middle range, so the situation is in the middle of its development. Because so much is going on, it will be difficult to say with much accuracy how they will ultimately resolve. However, the wands and swords present appear orderly: they are all upright, and none are clashing, or crossed, as in the 2, 3, 5, and 7 of swords or in the 5 or 7 of wands.

A few other things are apparent in the scan. The first and last cards are cups: the situation begins and ends in emotion. It appears to start in sadness and loss and end in happiness. But what happens in between? Also, the cups surround swords and wands, which are either neutral or weaken the cups, so the loss is not quite as bad, and the resolution is not quite as pleasing. Both experiences are lessened.

The top row shows a loss. The second and third cards are court cards, which can be read as two different people's reactions. Someone is lashing out very aggressively, and another is still contemplating what this loss means to them. These people are involved somehow in the situation Patricia finds herself in. I would read this row as the foundation of the situation.

The middle row makes an interesting picture visually. The first figure looks to the left, which is usually associated with the past. The middle figure looks to the right, associated with the present. The final figure looks off into the distant future. Patricia will gather her energy after this loss and decide what she wants to do. In almost no time at all, she will accomplish it and wait for the results.

The final row shows a respite from the situation. As Patricia rests, she will come into contact with someone who will help her finally resolve the situation in a way that pleases Patricia very much.

When reading the cards, one thing to notice is what is absent. Right away I noticed that there are the page, knight, and queen of swords, but no king. Intuitively, I'd say that this situation is about the loss of a leader in some project Patricia is working on. The knight and page are colleagues causing strife or disruption in the project. It seems to be a project rather than a job, as there are no pentacles present. The presence of cups does indicate it means something to Patricia on an emotional level.

The bottom line for Patricia is that she will do well to not interact with the disruptive colleagues. Instead, she should focus on what she wants and how she wants the project to play out. Once she's set those events in motion, she should step back from the situation, keeping her eyes open for someone who can advise or support her. And, in the end, if all remains as it is, she will get the end result that she desires.

Remember, these are just samples of how a reading can be done. No two readings will be the same. The reader, the querent, the question, the deck, the spread, and of course the circumstances of the situation are all variables in the equation and will all lead to different results. And as you try techniques suggested in this book, learn new ones from other sources, and invent your own, your reading practice will evolve into something completely unique—and hopefully very fulfilling and satisfying.

Conclusion

This phase of your journey is coming to a close, which means a new phase is about to begin. Like 0, the Fool, pack a little bag before starting out. I've heard that the road to enlightenment is long, so bring snacks and magazines. As you move forward on your own journey, take from this book only what you think you'll need or what pleases you. There is a whole tarot world out there waiting for you to explore it. If you have played with your cards and tried some of the exercises and activities, you have a good foundation and, ideally, the confidence in your skills, understanding, and beliefs to allow you to continue exploring.

Throughout this book, I've emphasized the idea that tarot has always changed and will always continue to evolve. Tarot started off as a game—something that you did for fun. Returning to those roots—to the ideas of playing and of fun—is what, ironically, helps tarot continue to grow. People just like you play with the cards and try new things. People run into problems or want to solve dilemmas, and so they arrange and rearrange the cards until they do. You are now part of those people.

Conclusion

Shuffle your cards. Play with them. Do something differently. Do something new. Ask hard questions. Ask crazy questions. Be part of not only your own future but also the future of tarot.

o The Fool

Appendix A

Suggested Reading

Sylvia Abraham, *How to Use Tarot Spreads*
Over three dozen tarot spreads. Can be used with any tarot deck.

Ruth Ann Amberstone and Wald Amberstone,
  The Secret Language of Tarot
A study of common symbols used in tarot cards. Theoretically can be used with any deck; however, is based on RWS.

Nancy Antenucci and Melanie Howard, *Psychic Tarot*
This book teaches tarot readers how to use their intuition to read the cards and how to strengthen their psychic abilities.

Ly de Angeles, *Tarot Theory and Practice*
Includes basic card meanings and a very interesting method of conducting a reading. Meanings are based on RWS, but the reading can be conducted with any tarot cards.

Josephine Ellershaw, *Easy Tarot Reading*

A fantastic explanation of how a reader weaves tarot card meanings into a seamless, useful interpretation. Available fall 2011.

Mary K. Greer, *21 Ways to Read a Tarot Card*

An excellent book for deepening your understanding of tarot cards. Can be used with any deck.

Mary K. Greer, *The Complete Book of Tarot Reversals*

A guide to understanding and using reversals in tarot readings using decks in the RWS tradition.

Elizabeth Hazel, *Tarot Decoded*

If you are interested in learning more about dignities and correspondences, this is an excellent resource. Can be used with any deck.

Kim Huggens, *Tarot 101*

A complete course in studying tarot cards to develop deeper meanings. Takes the unique approach of grouping cards by similarity of meaning rather than in numeric order. Can be used with any deck.

Corrine Kenner, *Tarot Journaling*

This book is out of print, but if you like journaling, try to find a used copy. It is filled with excellent journaling ideas. Can be used with any deck.

Llewellyn's Tarot Reader

An annual published from 2005 through 2008, filled with excellent articles, spreads, and deck reviews. Although all issues are out of print, used copies are on the market.

Teresa Michelsen, *The Complete Tarot Reader*
A self-study program for developing your own card meanings.
Can be used with any tarot deck.

Rachel Pollack, *Tarot Wisdom*
A fascinating journey through the tarot, based on Rachel's lifetime of studies, explorations, and musings. Can be used with
any tarot deck.

Appendix B

Suggested Decks in the RWS Tradition

If you have Internet access, it is very easy to find samples of images online. Local metaphysical shops sometimes have sample decks available.

The Gilded Tarot (also sold as Easy Tarot; Ciro Marchetti)
If you are interested in the Life Spread, get the kit called Easy Tarot, as it includes a book by Josephine Ellershaw that presents the Life Spread in greater detail. Computer-generated imagery.

Legacy of the Divine Tarot (Ciro Marchetti)
Computer-generated imagery.

Lo Scarabeo Tarot (Anna Lazzarini and Mark McElroy)
Clear, pleasing illustrations based on all three major tarot traditions: RWS, Thoth, and Marseille.

Mystic Dreamer Tarot (Heidi Darras and Barbara Moore)
Dreamy photocollage.

Mystic Faerie Tarot (Linda Ravenscroft and Barbara Moore)
Faerie-themed deck.

Pagan Tarot (Cristiano Spadoni Raimondo and Gina Pace)
Modern Pagan imagery.

Revelations Tarot (Zach Wong)
Cards are cleverly designed to be read both upright and reversed.

The Robin Wood Tarot (Robin Wood)
Pagan imagery.

**Shadowscapes Tarot (Stephanie Pui-Mun Law
 and Barbara Moore)**
Ethereal fantasy style.

Tarot of the Magical Forest (Leo Tang and Hau Chin Chun)
Charming, whimsical deck with forest creatures instead of humans.

Tarot of White Cats (Severino Baraldi and Pietro Alligo)
For cat lovers; the RWS featuring white cats.

Universal Tarot (Roberto De Angelis)
An alternative to the RWS; almost identical images in a different style.

Wizards Tarot (John Blumen and Corrine Kenner)
Images rich in lush art and Pagan symbolism. Available May 2011.

The World Spirit Tarot (Lauren O'Leary and Jessica Godino)
Linoleum block prints.

Websites with in-depth tarot deck reviews:

- aeclectic.net/tarot
- amazon.com
- llewellyn.com

Appendix C

Significators

To select a significator from among the court cards, first determine which suit best represents the querent, based on physical appearance, astrological sign, or personality. Then select the appropriate rank, based on age. One of the weaknesses of the traditional physical appearance method is that not every permutation of skin/hair/eye color is represented.

Physical Appearance

- Wands: fair skin with blond hair and blue eyes
- Cups: light to medium skin with light brown hair and blue or hazel eyes
- Swords: olive skin with dark hair and light eyes
- Pentacles: dark skin with dark hair and dark eyes

Astrological Sign

- Wands: Aries, Leo, and Sagittarius
- Cups: Cancer, Scorpio, and Pisces
- Swords: Gemini, Libra, and Aquarius
- Pentacles: Taurus, Virgo, and Capricorn

Personality

- Wands: a fiery, passionate, energetic person
- Cups: an emotional, sensitive, creative person
- Swords: an intellectual, logical person
- Pentacles: a down-to-earth, practical person

Age

- Page: a child or young woman
- Knight: a young man
- Queen: a woman
- King: a mature man

Appendix D

Correspondences

Learning tarot can be a lifelong journey. One of the reasons so many people love tarot is because it is a framework for nearly endless study and can be applied to so many areas of interest. As mentioned in chapter 1's "Tarot Fact and Fancy," in the eighteenth through twentieth centuries, tarot decks were used as placeholders for esoteric knowledge. The structure of a tarot deck lends itself so easily to so many modalities, such as astrology, numerology, or Qabalah. Connecting the tarot to other subjects or other ways of looking at the world has led to elaborate tables of correspondences. Correspondences are ways that things are associated with the tarot.

For example, the elemental energies discussed earlier are correspondences: fire corresponds to wands, etc. The cards, either individually or in groups/suits, have been associated with many, many things over the years: astrological signs, planets, seasons, numerology, Myers-Briggs personality types, Hebrew letters, Sephiroth (paths on the Tree of Life), colors, alchemy, musical notes, runes, plants, stones, directions, I Ching, and socioeconomic divisions, for example. In addition to all those associations (and more), different schools of thought sometimes assign the correspondences differently. There truly are no absolutes.

The lack of absolutes can make learning the cards feel like a daunting task. What you need to know, though, is that you do not need to learn or use any of these associations to read the cards. Using any correspondences should only enhance your understanding or add to your enjoyment of studying the cards. Explore them later, as trying to apply them now may only cause frustration. Here's why: while tarot does lend itself to other modalities, there is not one that fits absolutely and perfectly. Many times, some of the connections seem to make sense with the card meaning and image, and other times, the assigned correspondence seems to contradict the meaning—or worse, have no apparent connection at all. For people who enjoy studying and talking about tarot, this is not a problem; it only adds to the fun and interest.

Here is an example of the astrological and Qabalistic correspondences commonly associated with the Major Arcana. Note that this is not the only method of assigning astrological correspondences.

Major Arcana Card	Astrological Association	Hebrew Letter
0, The Fool	Uranus	Aleph
I, The Magician	Mercury	Beth
II, High Priestess	Moon	Gimel
III, The Empress	Venus	Daleth
IV, The Emperor	Aries	Heh
V, The Hierophant	Taurus	Vau
VI, The Lovers	Gemini	Zain
VII, The Chariot	Cancer	Cheth
VIII, Strength	Leo	Teth
IX, The Hermit	Virgo	Yod
X, The Wheel	Jupiter	Kaph
XI, Justice	Libra	Lamed
XII, Hanged Man	Neptune	Mem
XIII, Death	Scorpio	Nun
XIV, Temperance	Sagittarius	Samekh
XV, The Devil	Capricorn	Ayin
XVI, The Tower	Mars	Peh
XVII, The Star	Aquarius	Tzaddi
XVIII, The Moon	Pisces	Qoph
XIX, The Sun	Sun	Resh
XX, Judgement	Pluto	Shin
XXI, The World	Saturn	Tau

Minor Arcana Suit Correspondences

Note that these are commonly used but not the only ones used. In particular, I've seen many variations in the seasonal and directional associations.

Suit	Season	Direction	Time of Day	Medieval Humor
Wands	Spring	South	Noon	Choleric
Cups	Summer	West	Sunset	Sanguine
Swords	Fall	East	Sunrise	Phlegmatic
Pentacles	Winter	North	Midnight	Melancholic

Suit	Elemental Creature	Angel	Hebrew Letter
Wands	Salamander	Raphael	Yod
Cups	Undine	Gabriel	Heh
Swords	Sylph	Michael	Vau
Pentacles	Gnome	Uriel	Heh

Suit	Color	Gospel
Wands	Yellow	Mark
Cups	Red	John
Swords	Blue	Matthew
Pentacles	Green	Luke

Easy Tarot
Learn to Read the Cards Once and For All!

Josephine Ellershaw

"You don't need a special 'gift' to read tarot," insists Josephine Ellershaw. And to prove it, she has boiled down thirty years of experience into a straightforward, easy-to-use tarot guide for beginners. More than just a manual, *Easy Tarot* is a boxed kit that also includes the Gilded Tarot, a stunningly beautiful and popular deck by the well-known Ciro Marchetti.

Ellershaw gently guides novices to become proficient, sensitive, and responsible readers. Suit by suit, she introduces the distinct characteristics of the Minor Arcana, court cards, and Major Arcana. You will learn how the cards link to one another and produce insightful relationships as their unique energies merge in the Cross of Truth, the Celtic Cross, and other spreads. There is even a list of card combinations that commonly indicate specific events such as pregnancy, a wedding, a new job, and more.

A quick guide to card meanings, sample readings, safeguards, ethical guidelines, and tips for keeping a tarot diary are all covered in this well-rounded introduction to tarot.

- 978-0-7387-1150-8
- $19.95
- Boxed kit (5¼ x 7¾) includes the Gilded Tarot deck, a 240-page illustrated book (5³⁄₁₆ x 7⅝), and a layout sheet

---

Shadowscapes Tarot

Stephanie Pui-Mun Law;
text by Stephanie Pui-Mun Law and Barbara Moore

Renowned fantasy artist Stephanie Pui-Mun Law has created a hypnotic world of colorful dragons, armored knights, looming castles, and willowy fairies dancing on air—a world of imagination and dreams.

Lovingly crafted over six years, this long-awaited deck will delight all tarot enthusiasts with its wondrous blend of fairy tales, myth, and folklore from diverse cultures around the world. Featuring breathtaking watercolor artwork that fuses Asian, Celtic, and fantasy elements within the Rider-Waite structure, each exquisitely wrought card draws upon universally recognized symbols and imagery. A companion guide also presents evocative stories and insightful interpretations for each card.

- 978-0-7387-1579-7
- $28.95
- Boxed kit (5⅜ x 8¼) includes a 78-card deck and 264-page *Shadowscapes Companion* book